AF541735

PAX
IMPLICATIONS FOR
SIN
THE INDIAN DAWN
ICA

Praise for the Book

Pax Sinica is essential reading for all who are closely following the efforts made by Beijing to redesign the world order, and for those keen to understand India's determined and evolving bid to provide a compelling alternative.

—Stephen Harper, former Prime Minister of Canada

Are we entering a world ordered by China's interests, design and ambition? And how will India's rise, responses and propositions affect this contested world order in the decades to come? Few questions are more important in the world today, and few are as qualified as Samir Saran to throw much-needed light on them. This book will be a staple read for anyone interested in geopolitics.

—Carl Bildt, former Prime Minister of Sweden

Samir Saran and Akhil Deo offer an important Indian perspective on the most significant geopolitical feature of our time—the rise of China and its growing assertiveness. Coming amid the deepening political crises within the Western democracies and their weakening commitment to the post-War global order, China's rise confronts India with unprecedented challenges. *Pax Sinica* presents insights on how Delhi might navigate between the competing imperatives of political accommodation and strategic defiance of a powerful China on India's doorstep.

—C. Raja Mohan, Director,
Institute of South Asian Studies,
National University of Singapore

PAX SINICA

IMPLICATIONS FOR THE INDIAN DAWN

SAMIR SARAN
AKHIL DEO

RUPA

Published by
Rupa Publications India Pvt. Ltd 2019
7/16, Ansari Road, Daryaganj
New Delhi 110002

Sales Centres:
Allahabad Bengaluru Chennai
Hyderabad Jaipur Kathmandu
Kolkata Mumbai

ISBN: 978-93-5333-664-6

First impression 2019

10 9 8 7 6 5 4 3 2 1

Printed by Parksons Graphics Pvt, Ltd, Mumbai

For Shri Mukesh Ambani, with gratitude. His remarkable ability to anticipate the future, his steadfast faith in the youth and his unwavering belief in the rise of India are truly admirable and inspiring.

CONTENTS

INTRODUCTION

CHAIRMAN XI AND HIS VISION FOR PAX SINICA

For the past few years, our world has been in the midst of multiple disruptions. In the heady days of the post-Cold War era, few would have predicted the strain that the international system is experiencing today. In 2019, however, it is hard not to see the structural drivers behind these trends. Technological, political and economic winds have buffeted the norms and partnerships that have anchored the post-World War II international order. The forces of globalization have certainly created new winners—especially in Asia. However, they have also left behind many in the West. Power and wealth have diffused to an entirely new set of actors: from global cities and networked citizens to powerful corporations and malicious non-state actors. The ideas, frameworks, and institutions of the past are no longer sufficient for a new world. As the second decade of the twenty-first century comes to an end, the reordering of the world has only just begun.

Perhaps no other trend epitomizes the changing of the tides as much as the rise of China. The impoverished Asian giant of the twentieth century has transformed radically over the past forty years to emerge as a twenty-first-century superpower. China's miraculous rise can be traced back to Deng Xiaoping's decision to open its economy to the world, allowing foreign capital, skill, and technology to build domestic industrial capacity. Economic transformation was only one part of his legacy. At home, Deng carefully created a system of collective leadership that would guard against individual excess, and strongly advocated a peaceful role for China in international affairs, calling for the country to remain focused on its domestic development. This thinking paved the way for four decades of unstoppable growth. For the incumbent global powers of the day, China's foreign and economic policies seemed like a good deal. Western business could exploit labour arbitrage and outsource significant parts of their manufacturing requirements to China, while consumers benefited from lower prices. The economic value proposition that China offered was sufficient for the United States (US) and its allies to overlook working with what was otherwise a staunchly authoritarian and opaque regime. The political attention devoted to the erstwhile Soviet Union and then to a never-ending saga in the Middle East distracted from the rise of China on the world stage. The quiet growth of China suddenly became visible to the world in 2012. The country had a new general secretary, Xi Jinping, who unapologetically asserted the primacy of the Communist Party and looked to end China's 'humiliation' through a more aggressive foreign policy.

Xi was also aware that he was operating in a world order that was fundamentally different from that at the turn of the century. The global financial crisis in 2008 had exposed the fragility of Western capitalism, while the year 2016 had, in many ways, exposed weaknesses in democratic processes and institutions. Chairman Xi saw an opportunity in these disruptions—an opportunity to cement his place in China's history, and China's place in the conduct of world affairs. In addition to recognizing China's status as a political and economic superpower, once Chairman Xi had come to power, the world had to finally admit that the fundamental assumption about China's trajectory was based on an incorrect premise; economic liberalism would not bring about greater political freedoms. Indeed, as this book will show, China's economic miracle has only reinforced its unique brand of political authoritarianism and state-led capitalism.

THE RISE OF CHINA: A COMMON THREAD

Sitting in New Delhi in 2019, there are five stories that showcase Xi's unmistakable ambition and vision. The first story is that of the nineteenth National Congress of the Communist Party, which has undoubtedly already made its place in history. For Xi, it cemented his position as the most powerful Chinese leader since Chairman Mao. By christening himself as the 'core leader' who has injected 'Xi Jinping thought' in the Chinese constitution and abolished term limits for the post of China's president, not only has Xi firmly entrenched himself in the pantheon of China's ideological history, but he has also disrupted the principle of collective governance that has held the country in good stead. For China, the Congress laid out a more ambitious agenda for a 'new era' in which the nation is to become '...a global leader in terms of composite national strength and international influence' by the middle of the twenty-first century. Xi's promise to lead China into this new era has seen him double down on the primacy of the party, the need for indigenous technological progress, and a strong military. For the world, the nineteenth National Congress signalled a more assertive China. Moreover, it indicated Beijing's willingness to offer a new proposition for the world, which Xi called 'Socialism with Chinese Characteristics for a New Era'. Characterized by an effective blend of political authoritarianism and state capitalism, this was a model for organizing societies and the international system that China began significantly investing in.

The second story is of America's response to China's rise, epitomized by the clumsy arrest of Meng Wanzhou, Huawei's

Chief Financial Officer, in Canada on the ostensible charge of violating American sanctions on Iran. The real tensions, however, simmered under the surface—a new confrontation on politics, trade, and economics, with the tech sector being the beachhead. For the past five years or so, Washington has struggled to respond to China's rise. Under the Obama administration, much of China's aggressive behaviour, including its militarization of the South China Sea and its use of cyber espionage, we met by a reluctance to respond. This changed dramatically under the Trump administration. From labelling China a 'revisionist power' to tackling China's high-tech ambitions head-on, Washington has signalled its intention to recalibrate its approach to China. The Trump administration has concertedly targeted the Made in China 2025 Initiative, which the Middle Kingdom sees as key to its great-power ambitions. There is a belief in both Washington and Zhongnanhai that control over emerging technologies will determine the future of the world order. This contest between the world's two superpowers is central to the political realignments under way in the world. The resilience of American influence and the orbital pull of China's growth will continue to send tremors across the international system for decades to come.

The third story is that of the largest ever military exercises between China and Russia—the Vostok exercises. It was once unimaginable that Russia would invite the People's Liberation Army to its Far East, a region that has historically symbolized the centre of hostility between the two countries. It is worth recalling that as early as 2010, the Vostok exercises were a manifestation of Russia's response to China's rise. The war games and military drills were designed to keep a potential Chinese invasion at bay. In under a decade, both countries have come to embrace each other more closely, whether through cooperation in regional connectivity or partnership in matters of global governance. Most recently, both Moscow and Beijing conducted a joint aerial operation over islands in East Asia, another first for both powers, and an indication of deepening military cooperation. Today, the glue that binds them is a shared antagonism towards a Western-led world order. The two countries, however, do not necessarily have mutually compatible expectations from each other—Russia sees in China a counterweight to Western pressure, while China sees in Russia a partner to manage the security implications that will invariably arise along the Belt and Road Initiative (BRI). How these dynamics ultimately play out will be vital to defining the evolving political mergers between Europe and Asia.

The fourth instance to look to is Italy signing on to the BRI—the first G7 country to do so. The event demonstrated the depth of Chinese influence in Europe. For the past five years, Beijing has slowly chipped away at Europe's periphery—beginning with the 16+1 format that it incubated with the Eastern European nations. As in other parts of the world, China's massive investments under the BRI have weakened preexisting political alliances, allowing Beijing to upset and unsettle the sub-regional arrangements that have existed since the World War II. Xi has bet that the twenty-first century will be defined by the integration of the Asian and European continents. He is determined to ensure that the political, economic, and security dynamics of this process will be dictated by Beijing to serve its own interests. The symbolism of Italy joining the BRI is hard to miss. An ancient silk road once connected the Roman and Chinese civilizations centuries ago. The re-emergence of this route today, by Beijing's will and design, is a powerful signal of how political geographies are reorienting.

The final story is that of the Doklam standoff—an event that is, perhaps, the most significant escalation in Sino-Indian military tensions in nearly four decades. There are many complexities to sort through when analysing the standoff. At its core, however, the event was precipitated by a growing divergence between how China and India imagine the future of Asia. Looking ahead, there are multiple possibilities of what this event signifies. Optimistically, the events at Doklam will have compelled both China and India to reconsider whether conflict would serve either of their national interests. Alternatively, and more worryingly, Doklam could signal the beginning of a new phase in the relationship between the world's two most populous nations, where sharp tensions will punctuate periods of peace. It is unlikely that formal or informal summits, like the one in Wuhan, will mitigate the structural differences between the two powers. Most observers of international affairs believe that the US-China relationship will define the twenty-first century. This is partially true. However, it is also true that India will have emerged as one of the world's largest economies by 2050. This will be a phenomenal transformation for Asia and the world. Two Asian powers, both home to over a billion individuals, and both with fundamentally different domestic political systems and outlooks, will inhabit the same space. Thus, this relationship is bound to define and even transform the twenty-first century.

At first glance, each of these stories may seem unconnected. Yet the common thread running through them all is the rise of China. Each story adds up to a larger picture: a vision of a world ordered by China's interests, designs and ambitions. This book is an attempt at retrospection—a historical reading of how we got here and why. It is also an attempt to capture how India's rise, responses, and propositions will affect the incumbent world order. While the book will capture the dynamics of China's rise ever since the elevation of Xi Jinping, it will also explore how this phenomenon has implicated major actors, effected significant megatrends, and influenced the forcast of the future. How will American influence continue to affect the world? Does Europe have a future at all? What does Xi's consolidation of power mean for political stability in China? Can India emerge as a new guarantor of the liberal international order? The next nine chapters will attempt to answer these and other questions through a single prism: the rise of Xi and his quest for Pax Sinica.

I

A NEW ERA OF STRONGMAN POLITICS

The year 2012 marked the thirty-fourth year since Deng Xiaoping launched China's comprehensive reforms in 1978, committing China to a path of industrialization, market liberalization, and export-led growth strategy. The impact of these reforms on China was enormous. According to the World Bank Development Indicators 2011, the value of China's exports had reached levels that were 161 times higher than those of 1978, going from $9.8 billion to nearly $1.4 trillion.[1] By the end of 2012, China's GDP was roughly $8 trillion, making it the second-largest economy after the US. Indeed, by 2012 Deng's successor in the Communist Party headed a very different society and economy, at an unusually uncertain period in global politics.

Despite China's economic success, or perhaps because of it, by 2012 the country was structurally burdened by low-cost export-oriented manufacturing and was attempting to transition into a consumption-led economy. At the same time, China's leaders had to manage the social and economic disparity between the prosperous coastal areas, the rural hinterlands, and the peripheries. The Hu Jintao-Wen Jiabao era (2002–2012) was increasingly seen as a failure.

It was a period bereft of genuine economic reforms, for fears that this might exacerbate social, ethnic, and civil tensions. Within China, their rule came to be characterized as 'ten lost years.' In a scathing review in the *Financial Times*, David Pilling would write 'Mr Hu has not been bold… Perhaps hydraulic engineers rarely are.'[2]

Ahead of the eighteenth Party Congress in 2012, it was increasingly clear that Xi Jinping—who had been vice president since 2008—would take charge as general secretary of the Party. This was perhaps surprising if one considers Xi's own past.[3] When Xi was nine years old, his father, Xi Zhongxun, former head of the Communist Party's propaganda division, was expelled by Chairman Mao because of his disloyalty. Until then, Xi had grown up a 'princeling' in 'Zhongnanhai', the enclave of influential Chinese Communist Party (CCP) leaders. This was part of a sweeping 'Cultural Revolution' launched by Mao with the ostensible goal of purging Chinese tradition and Western capitalism to promote and preserve communist China. During the Cultural Revolution, when Xi was fifteen, his father was sent to prison and Xi was one of the nearly thirty million 'sent-down youth' who were forced to work in the Chinese countryside for 're-education' as part of Mao's 'Down to the Countryside' movement. He ended up in a remote village of the Shaanxi province where, Chinese state media often claims, he lived in a cave dwelling for nearly seven years. According to Xi himself, these seven years were transformative. 'When I arrived at the Yellow Earth at fifteen, I was anxious and confused,' wrote Xi in 1998, by which time he was a rising star in the Communist Party. 'When I left the Yellow Earth at twenty-two, my life goals were firm and I was filled with confidence.'[4]

Over twenty-five years, Xi rose through the ranks of the party leadership by performing well and keeping his disagreements to himself. His early career began in the northern province of Hebei, a relatively poor region, but he transferred quickly to the wealthier provinces of Fujian and Zhejiang. These regions were vital to Deng's 'opening up' policy, which saw China integrate with the global economy, and they would be important to Xi's career. It was here that Xi would learn about globalization and market reforms. Because of his known anti-corruption credentials, Xi was soon whisked off to Shanghai in 2007, which was then in the midst of a corruption scandal. He dealt with the matter so effectively that he was catapulted to the People's Republic of China's (PRC) central leadership that very year, and quickly became vice president of the country in 2008. Xi rose up the ranks as a clean, pragmatic, and pro-growth leader. According to a cable leaked by the Central Intelligence Agency (CIA), a well-connected Embassy contact referred to Xi, who was then a member of the Politburo Standing Committee and Vice President, as 'exceptionally ambitious', 'confident' and 'focused', and stated that Xi has had his 'eye on the prize' from early adulthood.[5] 'Unlike many youth who made up for lost time by having fun [after the Cultural Revolution],' the cable added, 'Xi chose to survive by becoming redder than the red.' It was these qualities that would come to define general secretary Xi.

THE CHINA DREAM

When Xi did take over as general secretary in November 2012, the expectations from his government were limited, and Xi himself remained somewhat of an enigma. Local newspapers painted him as a leader connected with the masses, who was 'amiable and easygoing.'[6] The Western media portrayed him as a 'compromise candidate';[7] as someone who had little real qualification to run China other than the fact that he belonged to the 'princeling' class and had few detractors. Kevin Rudd, the former Australian Prime Minister, wrote in 2012 that Xi was likely to have the same goals as all other Chinese governments since the Mao era: 'to sustain the political pre-eminence of the CCP within the country.'[8] There were signs that Xi himself was averse to being seen as overly ambitious. In an interview in the year 2000, Xi said, 'You always want to do something new in the first year, but it must be on the foundations of your predecessor. It is a relay race. You have to receive the baton properly, then run well with it yourself.'[9] However, the twelve years following that interview had apparently changed Xi's worldview quite significantly.

One of Xi's first public appearances as head of the Communist Party of China (CPC) was his visit to the National Museum of China in Beijing along with the new Politburo Standing Committee on 29 November 2012. Once there, he stood in front of a prominent art display titled 'The Road to Rejuvenation'. This display sits beside another famous showcase: 'The Century of Humiliation.' The story this display tells is one that every Chinese student learns early on in their education: In the mid-nineteenth century, China was humiliated by a series of outsiders, beginning with Britain, and then Japan. 'The Road to Rejuvenation,' on the other hand, narrates the victory of the Communist Party and its ideology—marking a return to the prosperity of the Chinese nation. It was here, at the end of the visit, that Xi Jinping spoke of the 'China Dream'—otherwise known as the great rejuvenation of the Chinese nation. Xi described the China Dream as achieving the 'Two Centenaries'. First, the economic goal of China becoming a 'moderately well-off society' by 2020, the hundredth anniversary of the CCP; and second, the goal of becoming a fully developed nation by 2049, the hundredth anniversary of the PRC.

RISE OF 'DADA' XI

To ensure that China could again find its rightful place in the world, Xi would have to undertake several structural reforms. Given that Xi's economic or political views were never widely published, opinions on his possible policy choices would vary widely. One op-ed for the *The New York Times* went so far as to argue that Xi would 'spearhead a resurgence of economic reform…and probably some political easing as well.'[10] While this may seem naïve in retrospect, Xi himself sent some positive signals. One of his first visits as head of the Communist Party was to Shenzhen in South China, which was once a remote fishing village and is now a thriving industrial region. The city is widely considered a shining symbol of China's embrace of market reforms. Here, he called on the country to 'tackle tough issues' and 'break free from the barriers of vested interest.'[11] The symbolism was not lost on anyone: Shenzhen was part of Deng Xiaoping's famous 1992 'Southern Tour', which sought to rally support for market-based reforms following the tumult of Tiananmen Square. Many believed that Xi was signalling a willingness to undertake the economic reforms that his predecessors did not have the political courage to manage.

On political reform, Xi once again gave reason for optimism. In December 2012, Xi declared that 'no organization or individual shall enjoy privileges beyond the constitution.'[12] He was giving voice to the popular angst against corruption that had plagued the Communist Party, a fact that even Chinese leaders were publicly acknowledging. In 2012, the Chinese Academy of Social Sciences published an anti-corruption bluebook, noting that corruption in China touches 'virtually all corners of society, from the economic, political and judicial fields to the social, cultural and educational ones.'[13] Transparency International's Corruption Perception Index 2012 ranked China as the eightieth most corrupt country out of 176. In January 2013, Xi Jinping publicly pledged to tackle this challenge by prosecuting both 'tigers' and 'flies'—in other words, high-ranking party officials and lowly bureaucrats alike. Xi understood perfectly well that corruption was undermining the legitimacy of the Party, and he was driven to change this reality.

More importantly, some argue that the anti-corruption narrative was also a useful tool to purge political rivals. Xi's ascent to the top job took place against the backdrop of corruption and espionage charges against Bo Xilai, the former governor and Communist Party chief of Chongqing province, who had been in line for an appointment to the National Standing Committee.[14] Soon after, *Xinhua* reported that Jiang Jiemin, the powerful head of the

State-owned Assets Supervision and Administration Commission (SASAC), had been removed from office on suspicion of serious disciplinary violations—Chinese doublespeak for corruption.[15] The official whose purge received most attention was Zhou Yongkang, the ninth most important member of the Chinese government and the country's chief of security and intelligence until his retirement.[16] Not surprisingly, what all these men had in common was their challenge to Xi's power.

By the end of 2012, Xi had purged thousands of party officials and acquired some extremely powerful positions for himself, including head of the Party and the military. In March 2013, he would also emerge as President of the Chinese state—merely a title, considering that he had already installed himself as head of several bodies overseeing the economy, military, internal security, foreign policy, internet governance, and so on. The Chinese press had taken to calling him 'Dada' Xi—or uncle Xi. This was a sign of exceptional reverence for any Chinese leader and an indication of Xi's consolidation of power.

In retrospect, it is clear why Xi would consolidate power in this way. In November 2013, the eighteenth Central Committee's Third Plenum Meeting would announce a comprehensive sixty-point blueprint for economic reforms. Xi was wary of the social implications of these reforms. In Xi's eyes, Western political ideals were responsible for unrest in China: whether it was Tibet in 2008, Xinjiang in 2009, or sporadically in Hong Kong. The Arab Spring in 2011 would only cement his view that the West was keen to export its ideology. In a leaked internal Party memo often referred to as Document No. 9, Xi called for the eradication of 'seven subversive currents' in Chinese society, including ideas such as Western constitutional democracy, universal human rights values, media independence, and civic participation.[17] Xi began to undertake mass line campaigns, reminiscent of the Mao era—going so far as to call them the lifeblood of the Party. He oversaw a reinforced ideological discipline in China's universities and cracked down on

China's blossoming social media ecosystems.

Many argued that Document No. 9 reflected the insecurities of Chinese society—and they weren't wrong. Xi understood that reforms would be painful, and gains would be slow. In his book *The Governance of China*, he wrote: 'We must be cognizant, especially during this new era of reform and opening up, that the Party will be exposed to unprecedented risks and challenges as China drives reform and opens up to a deeper level.'[18] However, Document No. 9 was also Xi's modus vivendi—he wanted to give the world a development model that did not rely on Western liberalism but was capable of delivering wealth nonetheless. For Xi, multiparty democracy is antithetical to both China's history and its economic development. 'We considered them, tried them, but none worked,' he once declared to an audience at the College of Europe in Bruges, Belgium.[19] He warned that the decision to abandon one-party rule could have catastrophic consequences.

THE BIGGEST PLAYER IN THE HISTORY OF THE WORLD

Despite the many domestic insecurities, Xi's most significant challenge to achieving the China Dream was the US. Soon after Barack Obama assumed the US presidency in 2009, Washington began signalling that it was preparing to turn its focus to Asia. America's 'back in Asia' policy was only reinforced by then-Secretary of State Hillary Clinton's 2011 announcement that the twenty-first century would be the US' 'Pacific Century'.[20] It was quite apparent that this policy was driven by Washington's desire to contain China's rise. Soon after, in 2012, defence secretary Leon Panetta revealed Washington's decision to re-posture its naval forces from a 50-50 split between the Pacific and the Atlantic to a 60-40 division respectively.[21] What truly irked Beijing was Obama's speech in Canberra during his Asia-Pacific tour, where he boasted that 'other models have been tried and they have failed—fascism and communism, rule by one man and rule by committee. And they failed for the same simple reason: They ignore the ultimate source of power and legitimacy—the will of the people.'[22] Obama was also forthright in his articulation of an Asia-Pacific order in which all countries, by which he meant China, would have to 'play by the rules.' He was not merely refusing to acknowledge what China believed was its right as an emerging power, but was also critical of its regime—a matter of high sensitivity to Beijing. To China, the message was clear, as reinforced by the country's official Xinhua News Agency: 'America's strategic move east is aimed in practical terms at pinning down and containing China and counterbalancing China's development.'[23]

Again, however, the world had underestimated Xi. Soon after graduating university, Xi worked as personal secretary to Geng Biao, who became defence minister after the Cultural Revolution—giving him unique insights into the workings of the People's Liberation Army (PLA), and allowing him to network with key leaders. After being named general secretary of the Party in 2012, Xi also quickly became Chairman of the Central Military Commission (CMC)—surprising many because of how powerful the post is, and the fact that outgoing Presidents generally hold on to it. He was earlier Vice Chairman of the Commission between 2010 and 2012 and played crucial roles in many of the commissions leading groups on the South and the East China Sea. Many of the tensions, analysts believe, could be directly attributed to Xi's hardliner attitude. His visit to the US in February 2012 as Vice President, where he called for 'a new type of great power relationship,' was a testament to how China now understood itself in world affairs. As Kissinger once remarked, 'China does not see itself as a rising, but a returning power.'[24] In other words, China's 'century of humiliation' was merely a historical aberration and its rise today as a great power is a return to the old normal.

Xi responded to Washington's 'Asia pivot' by strategically undermining the US' influence in neighbouring Southeast Asia. In

August 2013, China snubbed former Philippines President Benigno Aquino III, after he requested the US to increase military presence in the region, by refusing to let him visit Beijing for trade talks. Months later, China unilaterally declared a new in the East China Sea, forcing Japan and the US to scramble fighter jets and generally heightening tensions in the region. If Deng's maxim of 'setting aside disputes and pursuing joint development' continued to ring anywhere in Xi's thought process, his actions suggested otherwise. Instead, nationalism was Xi's calling card. Addressing the National People's Congress earlier in March that year, he called for the PLA to strengthen its ability to win battles.[25] Xi was making it very clear that the twenty-first century would not be America's Pacific Century—it would instead be about the China Dream. When asked what China's rise meant for the rest of the world, Lee Kuan Yew, Singapore's charismatic former Prime Minister, answered, 'The size of China's displacement of the world balance is such that the world must find a new balance.' China, he claimed, 'is the biggest player in the history of the world.'[26] And Xi, who was a true 'elitist' at heart, would spearhead the Communist Party's ambition of turning this into reality.

A RELATIONSHIP THAT WOULD DEFINE THE TWENTY-FIRST CENTURY

The rise of Xi Jinping's China Dream would also herald a new normal for the country's relationship with India—although this was not apparent at first. A few months after he became general secretary of the Communist Party, Xi wrote a letter to then Indian Prime Minister Dr Manmohan Singh which stated that 'China will, as it has been doing, pay great importance to developing relations with India.'[27] In an interview with *The Hindu*, Hu Shisheng, a South Asia scholar at the China Institutes of Contemporary International Relations (CICIR), read these signals as signifying that relations with India 'will be much more stable' under Xi, especially because

Xi Jinping would be busy 'addressing China's relations with West Pacific neighbours and China's relations with the US.'[28] Xi himself ostensibly confirmed this speculation a few months later in March 2013, when he met Dr Manmohan Singh on the sidelines of the Brazil, Russia, India, China and South Africa (BRICS) summit in Durban and declared that India was one of China's most important partners. Coming nearly a year after Xi's meeting with Obama, where he called for a 'new type of great power relations,' expectations were high in India that the new Chinese leadership would be keen to resolve the mistrust that had crept into the Sino-Indian relationship and seek a new type of relationship with India as well.

This enthusiasm was only bolstered by the fact that the new Chinese Premier, Li Keqiang, was due to visit India for his first foreign trip in May 2013—a sure indication of goodwill and momentum. Li, however, would be making a trip to a country that was steadily wary of China's ambition. In fact, a Pew Global Attitudes Survey recorded that in 2010, only 34 per cent of Indians held a favourable view of China, and by 2011, this percentage had decreased to 25 per cent. A full 35 per cent of Indians viewed their larger neighbour as a 'very serious threat.'[29] Indians had good reason to feel this way: On 15 April 2013, a day before Li would officially announce his visit to India, the PLA entered the Daulat Beg Oldi (DBO) sector in Depsang Valley in Ladakh, erecting tents and other such temporary structures. The Indian press was livid in its commentary, many drawing parallels to the border conflict in 1962. At the BRICS summit in Durban just two months earlier, Xi had reiterated his stand to Dr Manmohan Singh about the need to 'arrive at a mutually acceptable solution to the border dispute as soon as possible.' However, his actions indicated that Xi had not been all that serious.

The Indian administration was keen on downplaying the incident—after all, border incursions were a standard affair given the extreme differences in the perception of the boundary. While the PM referred to it as a localized problem, then External Affairs Minister Salman Khurshid called it 'acne' that could be addressed simply by applying an ointment. It took nearly twenty days of frantic telephone calls between government officials and several rounds of flag meetings on the border between military officers for the Chinese troops to finally withdraw.

What the Indian leadership perhaps missed was a more calculated heightening of tensions around China's periphery. The first sign of change, of course, was concerning the South China Sea. In 2012, at a study session of the Political Bureau of the CCP's Central Committee, Xi expressed his determination to see China emerge as a maritime power. The South China Sea, especially, was a part of what China's often refers to as its 'core interests'. While consistently dismissing the US' Freedom of Navigation operations in the South China Sea, Beijing saw the Indian Ocean as an open space for all actors. At the Sri Lanka-based Galle Dialogue in 2012, vice admiral Su Zhiqian of the PLA Navy was nonchalant in his assertion that the 'Chinese navy will actively maintain the peace and stability of the Indian Ocean.' Not only were the double standards blatant, but Beijing was also increasingly wary of a US-India entente—which was evident in Obama's speech in Canberra, where he explicitly acknowledged the potential of India as an Asian power. Defence secretary Panetta would later speak at the Institute for Defence Studies and Analyses (IDSA), calling India 'the linchpin for America's new defence strategy for rebalancing towards the Asia-Pacific.'[30] These were early indications of how Xi viewed his extended neighbourhood and its relationship with India.

All this talk of India becoming an Asian power must have amused Beijing, simply because China never considered India a great power—a forgivable thought, considering China's sheer size and the economic and military disparity between the two countries. At the beginning of the '90s, both India and China had economies of similar size and scale.[31] By the second decade of the twenty-first century, however, China was the second-largest economy in the world, five times larger than India, and spent nearly four times as much on defence. Even if the Indian economy was to grow by 9 per cent annually, it would still take decades to catch up to China. The trade relationship between the two countries was also indicative of the problem: while bilateral trade stood at nearly $66 billion in 2012, it was completely one-sided, with India's deficit amounting to $29 billion.

Economic imbalances aside, the Chinese were also quite contemptuous of those who believed that India provided an alternative development model to their own. Wang Yi, China's current foreign affairs minister, once called India's democracy 'tribal', and a 2013 *Global Times* editorial stated: 'By always defending itself as a democratic nation, India's general election and the rule of law can only constitute a well-recognized outer form instead of an inner force, because those democratic institutions have failed to bring about overall stability, equality and well-being to its citizens.'[32]

In many of its White Papers and Strategic Outlook documents, China would never place India on par with the US, or even Japan. Kevin Rudd wrote that 'within just thirty years, China's economy has grown from smaller than the Netherlands to larger than those of all other countries except the US.'[33] Even before Xi took charge, China was very aware of its newfound power—one that India had no credible claim to. It was unsurprising, then, that the *The New York Times* reported that under Xi, 'China's new foreign policy... will concentrate on consolidating what it considers the country's rightful place at the center of Asia.'[34] For Xi's China, India was merely a minor irritant, potent only to the extent that it could be used for American machinations in Asia.

Despite these emerging tensions, there was a surprisingly upbeat glow cast on Sino-Indian relations. Ultimately, neither country could ignore the sheer weight of history: In the fifteenth century, China and India accounted for nearly 50 per cent of the world's economic output, compared to Europe's 20 per cent.

Following near-simultaneous encounters with European empires, they would account for less than 10 per cent of the world's economic output by the middle of the twentieth century. Reportedly, Li stated that his visit to India was meant to tell the world that mutual political confidence between China and India was growing, practical cooperation was expanding, and that their common interests far outweighed their disagreements. Again, despite the border incident, when Dr Manmohan Singh visited China later that year, he spoke positively of the relationship, stating that 'when China and India shake hands, the world notices.' For the first time in more than five hundred years, China and India were reclaiming their wealth and power, and their relationship would define the twenty-first century. As we shall see in subsequent chapters, the fact that charismatic and powerful leaders would lead both states would only heighten the stakes.

II

A MULTIPOLAR WORLD WITH CHINESE CHARACTERISTICS

Xi Jinping's arrival was an inflection point in Chinese history. His narrative for China was undoubtedly popular at home: A nation once broken by the humiliation of defeat was rising to reclaim its legacy. It is essential to understand the global consequences of this narrative and the international climate in which Xi would execute it. By retracing some of Xi's early visits—specifically to the BRICS summit in Durban, South Africa, and his visit to Indonesia—a clear picture emerges of Xi's conception of the world order and China's role in it.

There were two important theoretical underpinnings in Xi's first attempts at diplomacy. The first was that China was enjoying a period of 'strategic opportunity'. In other words, the lack of external security threats would allow China to focus on domestic economic growth and engagement.[1] This assessment was validated not only at the eighteenth Party Congress, but also at the two preceding meetings of this body in 2007 and 2002.[2] Second, early in Xi's presidency, China was beginning to articulate a 'concept of major-country diplomacy'. Having leveraged its period of opportunity relatively successfully, the perception in China was that it must now employ its heft to fulfil strategic objectives in a manner that befits a great power. This idea was first given voice to by then foreign minister Wang Yi, who stressed that Chinese diplomacy would be more 'proactive' and based on a 'global perspective.'[3]

BRICS: MORE THAN JUST A TALKING SHOP

It was Xi's early visits abroad that allowed him to test some of these new conceptualizations of China's place in the world. One of Xi's first visits was to South Africa, to attend the fifth BRICS summit in Durban. By the time Xi took charge of the Communist Party, the BRICS itself had undergone a structural shift that was driven, in most part, by China's extraordinary economic growth. Speaking about this club over a decade ago, O'Neill was confident that Brazil and India were on the cusp of converging with China's economy. He believed that India had the most significant potential for growth among BRIC countries in that decade. He was, of course, mistaken. In reality, China grew more than twice as fast as the rest of the economies—while the remaining four never truly lived up to the expectations. By 2013, China's GDP was $1.5 trillion larger than the rest of the BRICS put together.[4] At the same time, China was, and continues to be, the largest single trading partner of Russia, Brazil, South Africa and India.

The 2008 financial crisis was a critical moment for BRICS, and specifically for China. Writing about the BRICS nations after the crisis, *The Economist* noted that the largest emerging markets were 'recovering fast and starting to think the recession may mark another milestone in a worldwide shift of economic power away from the West.'[5] For a group that was earlier considered a mere talking shop, the 2008 crisis provided the stimulus needed to institutionalize the BRICS' agenda of multipolarity. The statement released at the BRICS finance ministers, meeting in São Paulo in 2009 noted that though the crisis had to some extent affected all the BRICS countries, they displayed significant resilience. As Oliver Stuenkel argues, the BRICS not only insulated themselves from the crisis but also leveraged it as 'an opportunity to adapt global structures in their favour'.[6] He writes that the BRICS finance ministers met four times ahead of the G20 meeting in 2009 in an effort to influence the meeting outcomes. A group that had barely existed as an entity before 2008 was suddenly setting the agenda.

Thus, BRICS became immensely important for China, which, by this time, was revisiting its understanding of itself and the role it would play in the world order. Soon after the 2008 crisis, analysts in China were predicting an end to American unipolarity. An editorial for the *People's Daily*, for example, claimed that the US is 'no longer "King of the hill" in the coming multipolar world.'[7] By the time Xi became President, it was clear that the US was responding to this reality. In the past decade, China had grown into the second-largest economy in the world, but it still did not enjoy the levers of power that would allow it to influence international outcomes. At the same time, America's 'rebalance' in Asia was weighing heavily on Beijing. Gradually, territorial disputes, economic interests, and geopolitical manoeuvring were pitting two of the world's most powerful nations against each other. Hence, reliance on, and cooperation with, rising non-Western economic powers was essential to Xi early in his career.

RISE OF A NEW MODEL

For China, the BRICS was a perfect vehicle to realize its interests. Being developing countries whose importance was gradually rising, China could amplify their collective voice in world affairs. Ahead of his visit on 19 March, Xi told journalists that global governance must adapt to the 'profound changes in the global economic landscape' and ensure the representation of emerging economies.[8] Xi had a point—despite the rise of emerging economies, the Bretton Woods institutions, namely the International Monetary Fund (IMF), the

World Bank and to a lesser extent, the World Trade Organization (WTO), had remained obstinate in resisting reforms. Despite being a 188-member strong organization, the World Bank continued to be managed by the US and other Western powers. Contributing approximately $65 billion to the IMF, the US remained its largest shareholder and effectively wielded veto power over all deliberations.

China's frustration was understandable. In 2010, the IMF had decided to restructure shares in order to reflect China's growing weight in the international economy. Even three years later, however, the US had still not approved the reforms process. This stubborn behaviour struck a discordant vein with Chinese leaders, especially given that the world was more multipolar than ever before, a trend that even American intelligence agencies had pointed out repeatedly.[9] Consequently, Chinese leaders, and Xi specifically, stressed the need to democratize global governance. By 2014, Xi was speaking out about establishing a 'community of common destiny'. In its early avatar, the phrase captured two key ideas: the fragility of the existing international order and China's emerging propositions for global governance. In other words, Xi was calling for recognition of the fact that developing countries required a new framework for economic partnerships, one that acknowledged the realities of a multipolar world. As we shall discuss in later chapters, this phrase soon came to signify the entire gamut of China's economic and institutional statecraft—a process that began with the BRICS' New Development Bank (NDB).

NDB AND THE ERA OF MULTIPOLARITY

It was ultimately at Durban in 2013 that the BRICS decided to announce what *Foreign Policy* magazine called 'the only true significant outcome' of the group: an NDB. The NDB was intended to provide infrastructure finance to developing countries, while a new Credit Reserve Agency would provide liquidity assistance in the event of a balance of payments crisis. Calling this a 'significant outcome' was an understatement. For the first time since the end of the World War II, countries that were not part of the Organisation for Economic Co-operation and Development (OECD) were setting up credible and influential multilateral institutions. It was representative of the broader international system that Xi sought to achieve as part of his China Dream—in which Western powers were increasingly constrained in their ability to shape global outcomes.

Indeed, China's dominance in the NDB was obvious. For one thing, the Bank was headquartered in Shanghai. Also, while each BRICS country would contribute $10 billion to the Bank's capital stock, China would provide 40 per cent of a $100 billion Contingency Reserve Arrangement (CRA)—more than twice the amount of the other four countries. To many, it was odd that China would be keen on this initiative. After all, China already had its own development bank and a budget of nearly $200 billion for bilateral investment aid. In fact, by this time, China was paying more to the IMF than to the NDB itself. However, the NDB was essential to China insofar as it enabled Beijing to 'multilateralize' its diplomacy.

To understand why this was important to Beijing, it is useful to study China's evolving relationship with Africa. Over the past decade, Chinese firms have built infrastructure and transport networks across the continent. Chinese development banks have played a crucial role in their country's expansion—often offering better terms than Western financial institutions and bilateral partners. In a 2014 interview with the *Financial Times*, Ugandan President Yoweri Museveni was quite straightforward when asked why he preferred Chinese investment. 'They don't ask too many questions, and come with big money, not small money,' he said.[10] However, China's methods of doing business were also coming under greater scrutiny. In his book *China's Second Continent*, Howard French notes that China's state banks often offered loans that were tied to 'the use of Chinese companies, Chinese materials, and Chinese workers.'[11] African leaders soon began to take note of the implications of this reality, which cost China some political capital. The Governor of the Central Bank of Nigeria, Lamido Sanusi, wrote in a *Financial Times* op-ed piece that 'China takes from us primary goods and sells us manufactured ones. This was also the essence of colonialism.'[12] Other African leaders also started to regard China's investments with wariness. Indeed, Chairman Xi had to defend China's position in the NDB actively and insisted that China would not be a colonial power.

It certainly didn't help China that the US was actively cautioning developing nations about economic relations with Beijing. During a 2011 trip to Myanmar, which was enmeshed in an economic relationship with China, former US Secretary of State Hillary Clinton cautioned that the host country 'should be wary of donors who are more interested in extracting your resources than in building your capacity.'[13]

Thus, the NDB fulfilled multiple Chinese objectives. Firstly, this shift from bilateral to multilateral aid allowed China to insulate itself from a lot of the criticisms it had to face. Furthermore, it ushered in a new era of multipolarity—one that China would play a leading role in defining. It signalled a confidence that not only could Beijing provide leadership in institutionalizing alternative models of development, it could also seed the thought process for reorganizing the international financial system. The most prescient implication, however, was articulated once again by Jim O'Neill, who wrote, 'China's leaders may see a BRICS bank as a low-risk rehearsal for the role they are fated to play, in due course, at the International Monetary Fund and the World Bank, within the Group of 20 and maybe even at the United Nations.'[14]

GREATER PERIPHERAL DIPLOMACY

O'Neill, it appears, had underestimated both the velocity and the scope of China's ambition. The Chinese weren't interested in merely assuming leadership positions in established institutions—

they were prepared to create new ones altogether. In October 2013, the Obama administration was in disarray back in Washington and was fighting fires over a purported government shutdown. Xi, meanwhile, was on his way to the annual leaders' meeting of the Asia-Pacific Economic Co-operation (APEC) forum in Bali. Xi was already quite wary of Obama's 'pivot to Asia'—which by this time included a re-postured naval force as well as a new trade regime, the Trans-Pacific Trade Partnership (TTP), between industrial economies and many members of the Association of Southeast Asian Nations (ASEAN). Even before the APEC meeting, however, Xi was in Indonesia, making his mark as the first foreign leader to speak at its parliament. Here he announced that China would be launching an Asian Infrastructure Investment Bank (AIIB)—an announcement that would come to have global ramifications for the international order in the coming years. It was unsurprising that he chose to make this announcement in Indonesia. Soon after his trip, Xi chaired a meeting of the CCP's Peripheral Diplomacy Work Conference—a new work forum intended to improve China's diplomacy with its neighbours. As we shall see, it was also a forum that would allow China's economic statecraft to mature and complement its growing political muscle.

The establishment of the AIIB meshed perfectly with this strategy, allowing Beijing to shape a regional economic order and to deepen ties with its important neighbours. The idea behind the Bank itself was quite old. At the 2009 Bo'ao Forum for Asia—the Chinese version of Davos—a party official hinted that China was thinking of something along the lines of the AIIB, calling it 'a new Asian development bank to compete with Western-dominated institutions.'[15] The need to do this was only heightened after it had become apparent to China that the US was in no way interested in a changing power relationship—as Xi had found out during his trip to D.C. as Vice President.

With the AIIB, Xi was now toeing a different line. China 'cannot be bystanders and followers but must be participants and leaders,' he said at a December 2014 Politburo session, where he urged party officials to 'inject more Chinese elements into framing international rules.'[16] At the eighteenth Party Congress in November 2014, Xi had asserted that China was at a crucial stage of achieving the great renewal of the Chinese nation. 'In this stage,' he said, 'China's relations with the rest of the world are going through profound changes; its interactions with the international community have become closer than ever before. China's dependence on the world and its involvement in international affairs are deepening, so are the world's dependence on China and its impact on China.'[17] Indeed, this call for greater peripheral diplomacy was not simply an abstract concept. Feeling snubbed that the US was not responding positively to China's call for a new type of power relation, China was keen to expand its influence in Asia and undermine American interests in the region.

The reaction in Washington was immediate. While Asia was broadly welcoming about the new Bank, the US was suspicious of Chinese intentions. To the US, the call for a new Chinese-led multilateral development bank was a rude wake-up call. While earlier military showdowns in the South China Sea undoubtedly pointed to some tensions in the relationship, the AIIB was the first time that China's ability to reshape the global governance architecture became apparent. In 2005, US Deputy Secretary of State Robert Zoellick had called for China to become a 'responsible stakeholder' in an 'open, rules-based international economic system.'[18] Some would certainly say that investing in multilateral institutions was indicative of a responsible state. By late 2014, however, the US was engaged in a vigorous campaign to convince allies to reject Beijing's invitation to join the AIIB. US officials, according to the *The New York Times*, were asking pressing questions about how the new Bank would meet the standards of good governance and transparent financing.[19] Indeed, by the time Xi had announced his intention to launch the AIIB, the US was already finalizing the contours of the Obama administrations' 'pivot to Asia.' Unsurprisingly, many in the US saw the AIIB as an attempt to wean states in the region away from American influence before the 'pivot' was completed. Washington was concerned that Beijing's trade and investment initiatives would undermine American primacy in global finance and would lead to adverse strategic consequences for the US, and in 2015, US Treasury Secretary Jack Lew told the Congress that the World Bank and the IMF were critical parts of US national security.[20]

For China, the Bank itself served several purposes. Of course, Asia needed money—nearly $8 trillion for infrastructure and regional connectivity over the next decade, according to the Asian Development Bank (ADB).[21] It was not lost on observers that Xi was bringing something to the table at the APEC summit in Obama's absence. It undoubtedly helped Xi that despite the massive infrastructure needs of developing countries in Asia, the World Bank and the ADB—which were the two largest global financial institutions—did not possess the political will to fill this gap.[22] China's then finance minister, Lou Jiwei, asserted that the creation of the AIIB was China assuming more international responsibility for the development of the Asian and global economies.

ASSISTANCE WITH NO POLITICAL STRINGS ATTACHED

Despite what minister Jiwei would like us to believe, the AIIB was hardly a purely altruistic attempt to assist developing countries in Asia. China sought to expand its influence with the establishment of this Bank. The China Development Bank and the Export-Import Bank of China had already invested nearly $500 billion in Asia and Africa, more than the combined investments of the World Bank and the ADB. However, bilateral aid often gave rise to the accusation that political favours were being sought. Both the US and Japan had learnt this lesson, which is why they prefer to lend multilaterally. Studies have indicated that Tokyo explicitly uses its influence in the ADB to reward friends in the region. Two professors at Harvard University, Daniel Yew Mao Lim and James Raymond

Vreeland, for example, argued that 'Japan has leveraged its political influence within the Asian Development Bank (ADB) to facilitate favourable loans to countries useful for its broader foreign policy goals at the United Nations'.[23]

The proposed shareholding of the AIIB, with China holding nearly 30 per cent and wielding 26 per cent voting rights, already made it more dominant than the US and Japan in the ADB, who held a combined 25 per cent voting power. Chinese observers made no pretence about the fact that this would translate into de-facto control over the banks' activities. China had also learnt its lessons from Japan and the US well. AidData calculated that for every 10 per cent increase in voting support within the UN, China increased aid by an average 86 per cent.[24] It is not a stretch to argue that Beijing was merely doing what all great powers do: legitimize their quest for influence.

The AIIB, then, was Beijing's mechanism to provide alternate sources of loans to developing countries—pulling them away from Washington's economic orbit, while supporting its own foreign-policy initiatives. Indeed, both China and Xi have a long history of filling voids left by other powers. As early as 2009, when Xi was still Vice President, China had compelled Cambodia to deport dozens of Uighurs to be prosecuted for anti-government protests in Xinjiang. Even as the Obama administration responded to this alleged human rights violation by cancelling the supply of military equipment and financial aid, Xi arrived in Cambodia with $1.2 billion in loans—a figure that more than doubled by 2012. At the same time, Beijing was also willing to gain the upper hand by doing away with environmental and labour standards. Ever since Jiang Zemin and Zhu Rongji enacted a going-out strategy for Chinese companies at the turn of the century, they have become leading investors in developing economies blessed with natural resources. Their motto—don't mix business with politics—effectively allowed them to put aside many governance concerns. Indeed, during his trip to Africa just ahead of the BRICS summit in Durban, Xi boasted to his counterparts that Beijing offered assistance with no political strings attached.[25]

EXERCISING INSTITUTIONAL STATECRAFT TO ITS ADVANTAGE

Even though it was driven by a great power competition, the formation of the AIIB was not necessarily a fundamental rejection of the international order. Instead, the AIIB demonstrated China's diplomatic maturity in hedging its bets on global institutions. In fact, the AIIB has not necessarily threatened the international economic order as Washington had once feared. Instead, China remains invested in Western institutions like the ADB and even the World Bank. Nor has China employed the AIIB as a tool for geopolitical interests—India remains the largest benefactor of the AIIB. Instead, as Evan Feigenbaum convincingly writes, through the AIIB, China 'seeks to hedge its commitment to Western-led groups lest they fail to accommodate China's interest.'[26] Rather than compete on an institutional level with the West, the AIIB allows China to alter some of the rules of business, including investment standards, labour practices and so on. The Bank also legitimizes China's stake in the international economic order and buys friends and influence in developing countries. Ultimately, the AIIB makes it clear that China is now a great power and that it is capable of exercising institutional statecraft to its advantage, should the need arise.

Finally, the AIIB was also a crucial precursor to the BRI, a theme we will address in subsequent chapters. Thus, the reasons behind supporting initiatives with the BRICS and forming the AIIB signal China's intent to reshape the global order. It was preparing the institutions and aligning the actors. For years China's foreign policy had abided by Deng's maxim of 'conceal one's strengths and bide one's time', and even in 2008 it was unimaginable that the country would form institutions like the NDB and the AIIB. Under Xi, the

Chinese state, media and military were occupied with a new phrase, 'major power diplomacy', a term that highlighted China's growing confidence that it was already a pre-eminent global power. The AIIB fits neatly under this new conceptualization of China's grand strategy. As historian Howard French notes, 'The AIIB deserves this kind of historical significance not because it constitutes a threat to the US in any traditional or immediate sense, but because it represents more fully than anything else China's will to emerge, its bold coming-out and a demonstration of its resolve to become a powerful, across-the-board geopolitical actor.'[27]

Even as China was beginning to make its mark in global affairs, its neighbour, India, was preparing for elections in May 2014. By this time, the Indian electorate was tired of what they perceived as poor governance and corruption under the United Progressive Alliance (UPA), a coalition led by the Congress party. They ultimately voted for the Bharatiya Janata Party (BJP), led by Narendra Modi, an avowed nationalist and economic reformer. He would re-examine some of the foreign policy tenets that have defined India since Independence, and call for India to become a 'leading power.' This would eventually set India and China on a path of reinvigorated competition.

III

THE WORLD IS 'MODI'FIED

Even as Xi was consolidating power at home and abroad, India was preparing for its parliamentary elections—an event in which the world witnesses nearly 900 million people exercising their right to vote. By 2014, India was weary of the Manmohan Singh-led UPA. After a full decade in power, the UPA was crumbling under the weight of heightened voter expectations, allegations of corruption, and economic mismanagement. Capitalizing on this fatigue, the BJP came to power in May 2014 by winning an outright majority—a feat not accomplished in three decades. *'Saab Ka Saath, Saab Ka Vikas'* was Modi's rallying cry—a promise to revitalize India's moribund economy, raise living standards, and stem the plague of corruption that bedevilled the nation. Modi campaigned tirelessly, astutely employing legacy media and platforms like Twitter and Facebook to get his message across. Ultimately, his appeal lay in his ability to respond to the aspirations of a rapidly changing India.

Like China, India was also emerging as a regional power, albeit at a significantly slower pace. Until the 1990s, India's economic growth was laggard due to a burdensome and regulatory government—a vestige of the socialist principles that were popular among the political elite. After the reforms of 1991, however, India had grown by leaps and bounds, and its growing middle class had catapulted the country into the ranks of the world's emerging powers. While India's economic growth paled in comparison to China, India was already ahead of many G7 industrialized economies. Current estimates suggest that India is well on its way to becoming one of the world's top three economic powers by 2050, along with the US and China.[1]

The Modi campaign quickly caught on to the aspirations of a young, urban, increasingly global, and media-savvy middle class. It repeatedly emphasized the importance of generating economic growth and job creation to India's rise. As Ashok Malik wrote, Indians are now 'too well-off to be satisfied by an anti-poverty dole programme [favoured by the previous Congress government] but too poor to be genuinely middle class. They see themselves as socially underprivileged and their progress as thwarted by invisible social hierarchies that set up complicated, if not impossible, rules for entry—for professional advancement as much as political office—that usher in only the initiated.'[2] Once in office, the Modi government launched a slew of initiatives, such as Make in India, Skill India, Digital India, Startup India and Smart Cities, to remedy this error by enabling entrepreneurial activity, boosting manufacturing industries, creating jobs, enhancing skills, and improving production and livelihood standards.

And while India's growth will continue to be defined by these contradictions for some years to come, the fact remains that the country is rising at a time when wealth and power are diffusing eastwards. This will allow India to amplify its voice and agency in international affairs in issues ranging from trade, climate change, cyberspace, and security. India's agency will matter more and more as other developing countries in Asia and Africa, lacking secular social fabrics and stable bureaucracies, seek models to chart their development. If Asia is to be the defining geopolitical theatre of our times, then India's democratic credentials and relatively high rates of economic growth put it in a unique position to influence global affairs.

FOREIGN POLICY—A NEW CIVILIZATIONAL ROLE

The final year of Dr Manmohan Singh's government is best characterized as static. His government was perceived as either ineffective or absent when it came to responding to popular concerns, including the brutal rape and murder of a young woman in Delhi. To make matters worse, Dr Singh was battling a succession of massive scams across various sectors, ranging from defence procurement and coal allocation to spectrum licensing. The UPA was also lacklustre in terms of foreign policy. Despite some headway with the US following the civilian nuclear deal in 2005 and 2008, a fractured coalition government made it impossible to build a domestic consensus on crucial foreign-policy issues. For example, Mamata Banerjee, the chief minister of West Bengal, effectively scuttled any real possibility of a land boundary sharing agreement with Bangladesh, while the Dravida Munnetra Kazhagam (DMK), a regional party in Tamil Nadu, prevented strategic relations with Sri Lanka. Pakistan remained a thorn in India's side, especially following the 2008 Mumbai terrorist attack. And much to the chagrin of India's young population, China's incursions into the Himalayas were continuing uninterrupted. Furthermore, following the 2008 financial crisis, there was a tendency to resort to populist economic policy, slowing the pace of reforms. C. Raja Mohan insists that because of these trends, 'there was a renewed temptation to adopt the earlier notions of non-alignment defined in anti-Western terms, a reluctance to seize the new possibilities for economic and strategic cooperation with the US and hesitation in resolving problems with neighbours.'[3] Others were more critical in their assessment, comparing Prime Minister Manmohan Singh's two terms to the Hu Jintao regimes, or the 'lost decade' in China.[4]

This is not to say that observers or citizens had any real

sense of the BJP's foreign-policy priorities. It didn't help that the BJP's election manifesto itself had very little to say about foreign policy, which was discussed in less than two pages of the entire document. It promised to 'fundamentally reboot and reorient the foreign policy goals, content and process in a manner that locates India's global strategic engagement in a new paradigm.'[5] Despite this bold proclamation, there was some scepticism about Modi's expertise in foreign affairs. In the run-up to the general elections, Manjari Chatterjee Miller argued in *Foreign Affairs* that Modi was unlikely to change 'the broad shape of Indian foreign policy,' which has remained 'the same for nearly five decades.'[6] Even when shifts do occur, she writes, they are not 'sudden', 'have rarely, if ever, been political,' and 'have had little to do with the Prime Minister's political ideology.'

By the time Modi took charge in 2014, the world around India was changing rapidly. Freed from the complex dynamics of the Cold War in 1990, India had benefited from economic integration and collective security, largely guaranteed by the US. The set of economic reforms pushed through by then Prime Minister Narasimha Rao and then finance minister Manmohan Singh launched India on a path of sustained economic growth for nearly two decades. Like in China, India's rise, in many ways, was a correction of a historical error. For millennia, wealth, cultural power, economic innovation and technological accomplishment lay in Asia. Only in the fifteenth century did the gap between the West and the rest begin to widen dramatically—followed by the Industrial Revolution and the colonization of Asia and Africa. China's steady rise, accompanied by the tiger economies of South and East Asia and followed closely by India, were undoubtedly crucial moments in history. They signalled that the days of Pax Americana were numbered, and this shift in the global balance of economic power would bring with it significant political and military consequences. Modi was quick to grasp this reality. 'We are not living in the eighteenth or nineteenth century. We are living in the twenty-first century,' he claimed in an interview.[7] He was also critical of the dysfunction evident in India's administration, promising to 'put our own house in order so that the world is attracted to us.' Modi saw a new 'civilizational role' for India, one built on India's ancient traditions and taking advantage of its economic capacity and relative security.

In light of these factors, Gideon Rachman posed the following questions for the Modi administration: 'Should India continue to define itself, as it did during much of the Cold War, as a leader of the Global South—the poorer countries of the world that believed themselves to be disadvantaged and exploited by the industrialized nations of the North? Or should India see itself as part of the rising East—an Asian nation that is poised to correct the historic injustices and power imbalances that were imposed during the centuries of Western imperialism?'[8]

BRIGHT HOPE FOR SUSTAINING ASIAN DYNAMISM

India's foreign policy would indicate a nation that was finding the balance between being a leader of the Global South and seeking to correct the damage done by Western imperialism. Two aspects of PM Narendra Modi's foreign policy stand out the most in this regard.

The first is that his administration has made it clear that India will play a role in shaping the Asian century. Speaking to an ecstatic Indian diaspora in Madison Square Garden in September 2014, Modi claimed that 'The world is convinced this is Asia's century… others assert it is India's century. It's not an empty claim. India has the potential.'[9] India's vision for Asia began with its own neighbourhood. When Modi took his oath as the fourteenth Indian Prime Minister in May 2014, he generated much excitement among observers of Asian politics by inviting the heads of state of India's neighbours for his swearing-in ceremony. Soon after, Modi visited each of India's immediate neighbours, beginning with Bhutan and going on to countries like Sri Lanka and the Seychelles, which saw the first bilateral visit from an Indian Prime Minister in over two decades. Delhi had long cherished its primacy in South Asia—as the largest country in the region by any metric, India saw itself as the architect of the region's order. Successive foreign-policy blunders by previous governments, however, made this a questionable claim. And China's rapid inroads into South Asia were slowly pulling the region's states away from Delhi's political and economic orbit. Indeed, Modi was well aware that India's economic growth and development could not be fulfilled without its neighbourhood. Nor could India influence pan-Asian outcomes if it remained mired in minor disputes with its neighbours. Modi's reinvigorated outreach sought to address both these challenges.

Modi's South Asian diplomacy was merely the beginning. During his first visit to the annual ASEAN summit in November 2014, the Modi administration announced that India would no longer 'Look East', a policy primarily driven by economic need, but would now 'Act East', signalling an intention to establish more strategic ties with ASEAN members. Once again, Modi emphasized the rising importance of Asia, claiming during his visit to Singapore that 'the re-emergence of Asia has been the greatest phenomenon of our era.'[10] India's eastward push made good strategic sense. The Southeast Asian countries were hotbeds of innovation, finance, and technology, and therefore would soon be hosting a major portion of the world's wealth. At the same time, this region was home to two-third of the world's population and, more importantly, another rising power—China. The Modi administration was not simply keen on integrating India with its periphery, but also shaping its governance architecture. For Modi, the most critical need in Asia was to uphold and strengthen the rules and norms of collective behaviour built on the consent of all rather than the strength of a few. He insisted that India would 'work with countries in the region and beyond...to ensure that the commons—ocean, space and cyber—continued to remain avenues of shared prosperity, and not become new theaters of contests.'[11]

Later in 2015, Modi toured the five Central Asian Republics (CAR) of Uzbekistan, Kazakhstan, Turkmenistan, Kyrgyzstan, and Tajikistan to reinvigorate the 'Connect Central Asia' strategy launched under the Manmohan Singh administration in 2012. India's interests in Central Asia manifested through Iran, where it was investing in the strategically located port of Chabahar. This port formed the southern end of the International North-South Transport Corridor (INSTC), a multination rail, road, and shipping network connecting India with Russia via Central Asia. During his speech in Kazakhstan, Modi said, 'Our hopes of an Asian Century will be realized when we see Asia as one, not as South, West, East, or Central.'[12]

In his book, *Five Rising Democracies and the Fate of the International Liberal Order*, Ted Piccone of the Brookings Institute wrote that Modi's first year in power displayed his willingness to take initiative in South Asia and the broader Asian theatre.[13] As mentioned earlier, Modi's Asian focus was different from previous efforts by India to integrate with the neighbourhood. Earlier efforts were driven either by the need to demonstrate Indian leadership in a particular geography, or were manifestations of South-South solidarity, or were necessitated by security concerns emanating from across the border. Modi's Asian thrust, on the other hand, was a quest to find new partnerships, both in terms of finance and technology, to invigorate India's development trajectory and to make India's voice more prominent in the twenty-first century. The move was, in some ways, an explicit recognition of the fact that the Atlantic countries did not have the financial capacity to invest in large infrastructure and energy projects, or the wherewithal to offer twentieth-century inputs, including equipment, energy and technology, for an insatiable India.

India was well aware that the distribution of wealth and power was at once benefiting India while changing the dynamics of actors in the region and the world. At the same time, Modi recognized that the success of the Asian century would depend on countries in the region escaping the artificial geographic boundaries that separated South, Southeast, and Central Asia. This was prescient insofar as the economic and political forces which were already organically linking these regions together were concerned. In the late twentieth century, US Secretary of State Henry Kissinger recognized that India would emerge as a crucial swing state in the post-Cold War international order. Writing in his book *Diplomacy*, he predicted that India's 'geopolitical interests will impel it over the next decade to share some of the security burdens now borne by the US in the region between Aden and Malacca.'[14] These are the very regions Modi would prioritize in his first year in power.

ESTABLISHING INDIA AS A GLOBAL POWER

Articulating a vision for India in the Asian century was only one of Modi's major foreign-policy shifts. The second plank that would build on India's influence in Asia was making India a leading power. Less than a year after he took office, Modi challenged his senior diplomats to help India position itself in a leading role globally, rather than as just a balancing force.[15] This ambition was elaborated by then foreign secretary S. Jaishankar when he spoke of the 'greater confidence, more initiative, and stronger determination' that was defining India's foreign policy.[16]

By this point, India was already the seventh-largest economy in nominal terms, and more integrated with the world than ever before, with nearly 40 per cent of its GDP linked to global trade. Achieving India's key foreign-policy objectives, stability for higher economic growth and peace in the region could no longer be fulfilled without greater Indian engagement. It was, therefore, time to ask whether India should raise its level of ambitions. Was Delhi content to react to events, or should it be shaping them too—on occasion even driving them? This imperative was hardly a domestic issue alone. Countries in the region and around the world were keen for India to shoulder larger responsibilities to facilitate global economic integration and strengthen regional security cooperation. This was especially crucial at a time when the post-war order was strained because of a changing balance of power, exacerbated by the 2008 global economic crisis. Jaishankar summarized these aims succinctly when he stated, '[Insofar] as larger international politics is concerned, India welcomes the growing reality of a multi-polar world, as it does, of a multi-polar Asia.'[17] Put simply, the Modi administration's intention was that India would make foreign policy choices to accommodate itself in the existing order, shape and influence regional and global outcomes, or create new space to establish its presence as a global power.

The phrase 'leading power' was a modest articulation of India's great ambitions. Three trends in Modi's early career establish these ambitions. The first, as Professor Ian Hall points out, was India's rise as a normative power.[18] He highlights that Modi has focused on the importance of 'democratic values' not only in countries like Japan and the US, where such rhetoric is generally welcome, but also in Bhutan, Nepal, Afghanistan, and Sri Lanka, and in institutions like the United Nations (UN). Democracy was far from the only norm that India was articulating. It was engaging more with conversations on cyberspace, maritime security, and trade and connectivity through the prism of multilateralism and rules-based cooperation. Second, India was beginning to take a more active role in global governance—a great example of which was its role at the Paris Climate Change Summit in 2015. Traditionally, India fought for more carbon space for developing countries to industrialize, a reflexive 'North-South' stance that was embedded in Indian elite thinking. However, Modi chose to abandon this narrative, instead committing to the process by setting substantial national contributions. In doing so, he demonstrated India's willingness to take leadership in responding to emerging global challenges. Finally, India under Modi was also willing to embrace pragmatic partnerships with larger powers, especially the

US, which would support its rise. The two summits between Modi and Obama, one in September 2014 and one in January 2015, served to both arrest the drift in their relationship and set the stage for building a more strategic partnership, in a future where Asia would determine the architecture of the twenty-first century.

In his 2015 book, *Modi's World: Expanding India's Sphere of Influence*, C. Raja Mohan argued that Modi had ushered in a 'third republic' in the context of India's foreign policy, which included, among other things, a more empowered Prime Minister's Office (PMO), a willingness to discard naïve notions of non-alignment and strategic autonomy, and the political will to discard a reflexive anti-America streak that otherwise characterized India's foreign policy elite.[19] With a firm mandate at home, Modi was well placed to chart a new direction for India's foreign policy, positioning it as the fulcrum of the realignment of powers that would play out in the twenty-first century. However, India would prepare for a more complicated relationship with its larger neighbour, China—a country with an equally powerful political leader and far grander ambitions.

THE CHINESE DRAGON AND THE INDIAN ELEPHANT MOVE TOWARDS MULTIPOLARITY

Beijing lost no time in reaching out to Modi. Less than a week after he was inaugurated as Prime Minister, Premier Li Keqiang called Modi to convey that China viewed India as a development opportunity and that it was willing to enhance mutual trust. Within a month, foreign minister Wang Yi visited Delhi in June of 2014 as Special Envoy of the Chinese President and praised Modi for injecting a 'new vitality into an ancient civilization.'[20] Even as China was embroiled in territorial disputes with its neighbours, it seemed keen to ensure that India was not drawn into these disputes. Yi, in fact, indicated that China was willing to consider a final settlement of its land-border disputes with India and was prepared to invest more in its neighbour.

Beyond the diplomatic rhetoric, however, it was clear that Modi came to power at a time when Xi was ushering in a period of greater Chinese assertiveness abroad. China's economic rise was enabling the country's westwards and southwards expansion in an effort to stretch its influence and secure its interests. This expansion was both economic and political. In January 2014, a few months before Modi became Prime Minister, a Chinese naval group entered the East Indian Ocean through the Sunda Strait before returning to the Pacific, marking the first time that China conducted such an unannounced exercise in the Indian Ocean.[21] At the same time, the BRI, Xi's signature initiative, was entangling India's neighbourhood in economic dependency with Beijing. In Bangladesh, for example, China had overtaken India as the country's largest trading partner as early as 2005, supplying key garment inputs without any customs hassles. Between 2009 and 2013, China was the source of 82 per cent of Bangladesh's arms purchases, according to the Stockholm International Peace Research Institute (SIPRI).[22] Similarly, in Sri Lanka, China had provided economic and military assistance along with diplomatic cover to the government, allowing it to successfully wage a civil war against the Liberation Tigers of Tamil Eelam (LTTE), an insurgent group. While India and Western powers were unwilling to provide this support, given the human rights situation in the country, China emerged as Sri Lanka's biggest source of foreign direct investment (FDI) and a leading provider of development loans for projects such as the Hambantota Port, a strategic piece of infrastructure in the Indian Ocean. Having already perfected this playbook in East Asia, where China's economic relations with the ASEAN combined with its militarization of the South China Sea was creating disruption to accommodate China's rise, Xi was apparently keen on testing this strategy in the Indian Ocean.

New Delhi was well aware of this reality. As former foreign secretary Shyam Saran noted in 2015, China was rapidly constricting India's space for diplomacy through its economic and diplomatic relationship with India's neighbours.[23] In fact, China featured quite prominently during Modi's campaign trail. At a book launch event in 2013, Modi remarked that India was making a mockery of itself with its limited and timid approach to China. On the campaign trail in February 2014, Modi visited Arunachal Pradesh, a province China has tried to claim, and declared that no power on Earth could snatch it away.

Indeed, Modi's early efforts at shoring up neglected relationships with India's neighbours were in many ways efforts to contain China's expansion into the region. During his trip to Bangladesh, an agreement to end a long-standing border dispute with the country was seen as a key facilitator of trade and good relations. Soon after, Mahinda Rajapaksa was defeated in Sri Lanka—news that was greeted with much delight in New Delhi considering his pro-China stance—and Modi became the first Indian Prime Minister to pay a bilateral visit to Sri Lanka since 1987. Similarly, upgrading India's Look East policy to Act East supported India's ambition of deepening defence and strategic cooperation with countries like Japan and Vietnam. At his speech in Tokyo in September 2014, Modi made a less than ambiguous reference to China's aggression in the South China Sea, criticizing 'an eighteenth-century expansionist mind-set' that allows for 'encroaching on another country, intruding in others' waters, invading other countries and capturing territory.'[24] Given Modi's early policy towards the neighbourhood and Southeast Asia, Linda Jakobson and Rory Medcalf saw in these initiatives an 'increasingly coordinated and resourced set of policy responses aimed at limiting China's influence and presence in the Indian Ocean.'[25]

Given these realities, Xi's visit to India came at a crucial time—right after Modi's visit to Japan, and just before his visit to the US. Ahead of Xi's visit in September 2014, he authored an op-ed in *The Hindu*, noting that 'as two important forces in a world that moves towards multipolarity… [The] Chinese Dragon and the Indian Elephant both cherish peace, equity and justice.'[26] Xi's willingness to embrace a multipolar Asia, however, was questionable. On his way to visit India, Xi first stopped over at the Maldives, the tourist archipelago where China's economic influence has been growing steadily, followed by a visit to Sri Lanka, where China has become the largest investor. Both visits were unmistakable signals of China's rising power in India's neighbourhood.

Modi definitely sees China as a rival power, but he also realizes that the balance of power is heavily tilted in favour of Beijing. India's economy is dwarfed by China's nearly five times larger GDP. China knew full well that Modi's India was looking for new sources of finance and technology, and Xi's visit was intended to respond to this appetite. An article in the *Global Times* highlighted that Modi was ready to do business with China, even going so far as to suggest that Modi would become 'India's Nixon' given his right-wing background.[27]

In a desire to build on this economic convergence, New Delhi even broke protocol by inviting Xi to Ahmedabad, the capital city of Gujarat, where Modi was previously chief minister. Here, they exchanged platitudes familiar to observers of Sino-Indian relations, with Xi calling India ancient and enchanting, while Modi reminded visiting journalists that Chinese technology was responsible for sugar being called 'cheeni' in India. This bonhomie was, unfortunately, soon shattered as Xi's visit was soon overshadowed by an ill-advised three-week PLA incursion across the disputed border in Ladakh. Unsurprisingly, the visit itself eventually produced very few tangible outcomes.

The parallels between the 2014 border incursion and the standoff at DBO in April 2013 during Premier Li Keqiang's visit to India were unmistakable. The difference in 2014, however, was New Delhi's reaction. India mobilized three battalions of troops—nearly a thousand soldiers—in the disputed site. Rather than play down the issue, Modi was also blunt about this incident in a press conference with Xi, during which he raised India's serious concern over repeated incidents along the border.[28] He even went on to state that peace on the border was a prerequisite for good relations, as opposed to earlier positions that put the dispute on the back-burner. In an interview a few weeks later, General V.K. Singh, minister of state for external affairs, pointed out that this was a concerted effort to take a stronger stance on China's aggression. 'If you keep giving a concession, it only perpetuates the problem,' he said, adding that 'somewhere up the hierarchy someone has to say let's hold on.'[29]

China's motivations, however, were never apparent. Unexplained Chinese military activity on the disputed border was only ever likely to leave most Indians hostile rather than keen on partnerships. Already, the public attitude towards China was quite bleak. A 2013 Lowy Institute poll showed that 83 per cent of Indians considered China a security threat, while 70 per cent thought China's goal was to dominate Asia.[30] If the goal was to either signal disapproval about the new administration's hard-line stance on China, or to develop partnerships with Tokyo and other regional powers, it never truly had the desired effect. It certainly did not help that within a week of Xi's India visit, he addressed the PLA and exhorted them to be prepared to win a regional war.[31]

The fact that these events took place just before Modi was set to visit Washington only eased the way for him to develop a closer partnership with the Obama administration. China's nationalist media, meanwhile, trumpeted the 'inferiority of India's democracy', arguing that India was not a 'first-class major power' and was being drawn into American and Japanese machinations to contain China. The border incursion, if anything, certainly helped the Obama administration engage with India more on the question of Asian security. During Obama's 2015 visit to New Delhi as the first ever American guest of honour at India's Republic Day parade, 'the first 45 minutes were dominated by just one topic: China', with the Obama administration finding that 'Mr Modi's assessment of China's rise and its impact on the greater strategic situation in East Asia was closely aligned with their own.'[32] India and the US went on to sign a joint statement criticizing Beijing for provoking conflict with neighbours over control of the South China Sea; and even agreed on a 'Joint Vision for the Asia Pacific'—an early indication of India's desire to take on a greater security role in the region.

At the end of his visit to India, Xi contended that only when the China-India relationship developed would a real 'Asian century' emerge. For both India and China, a change in leadership was significant. Xi and Modi had replaced leaders widely seen as lacking political charisma, both found nationalism a useful tool in statecraft, and both were seen as the most powerful political leaders in decades. This leadership transition also took place at a critical moment in history. As the US National Intelligence Council Report correctly predicted in 2002, the most pressing challenge for the international community would be confronting the near simultaneous military, political, and economic rise of China and India.[33] At the same time, it was becoming clear that the Indo-Pacific region and the Eurasian landmass would be at the centre of global trade and conflict. It is here that the interests and influence of China and India would overlap—revealing the contours of the twenty-first century's great power dynamics.

IV

BELT AND ROAD INITIATIVE: A COMMUNITY OF COMMON DESTINY

By 2014, both India and China had begun to articulate a new role for themselves in a world order that was changing rapidly. Even as India desired to become a leading power, Xi had exhorted China to embrace 'major-country diplomacy'. Between the two countries, however, China almost certainly had taken the lead in defining its vision for the world. A year after Xi Jinping assumed the presidency, he would announce a project with far-reaching consequences: the One Belt One Road Initiative (OBOR).

The OBOR initiative first garnered attention in 2013, when Chairman Xi visited Kazakhstan intending to break the bottleneck in Asian connectivity. He announced that China would build a sprawling network of infrastructure projects including highways, railways, and energy pipelines—both southwards, through Pakistan and India, and westwards, through the landlocked Central Asian states, and onwards through the Persian Gulf and on to Europe. The Silk Road Economic Belt, as Xi named it then, would 'open the strategic regional thoroughfare from the Pacific Ocean to the

Baltic Sea, and gradually move toward the setup of a network of transportation that connects Eastern, Western and Southern Asia.'[1] Soon after, he addressed Indonesia's parliament—a first for any foreign leader—where he announced plans for a 'Maritime Silk Road (MSR)', linking China's prosperous coastal provinces with Southeast Asia along with the Indian Ocean littorals, ultimately culminating in Europe.[2]

In both speeches, Xi also highlighted China's historical patterns of interaction with these regions, crediting the Han envoy Zhang Qian with establishing the Silk Road and new patterns of East–West communication networks in Kazakhstan, and praising Zheng He, a Ming dynasty admiral, for bequeathing 'stories of friendly exchanges between the Chinese and Indonesian peoples' in Bali. Together, the two projects would connect three continents and two oceans—Asia, Africa and Europe, through the Indian and Pacific Oceans—with transport and communication infrastructure funded and built by China. One Belt One Road, as the project would come to be known initially, involved over sixty countries with a combined population of over four billion people and whose markets accounted for about one-third of global GDP. Since the announcement of this multitrillion-dollar project, much speculation has surrounded the impetus behind China's ambitious infrastructure drive and the consequences of it. Publicly, China cites an ADB estimate that the broader Asian region faces a yearly infrastructure financing shortfall of nearly $800 billion,[3] a yawning gap that China was prepared to fill. A second reason was securing energy supplies through the Central Asian landmass, which was both an economic and a strategic imperative. For years, Chinese strategists have split hairs over the 'Malacca dilemma'. In other words, the risk that, in the event of a major military confrontation, hostile powers could easily bottleneck the Malacca Straits located along the Indonesian archipelago, which is China's primary gateway for sea lines of communication (SLOC), trade, and energy routes. Building energy pipelines through the Asian continental realm obviated this risk. Third, the OBOR could address some of China's domestic economic priorities. Most of China's state-owned enterprises were burdened by overcapacity in key industrial sectors such as iron, steel, cement, and aluminium. The OBOR allowed China to fund overseas commercial operations that create demand for its industrial products and outlets for its vast labour force. Fourth, China's westward expansion would afford it the opportunity to develop its frontier provinces—Xinjiang and Tibet—which are otherwise plagued by frequent social unrest.

The fifth reason for OBOR was geopolitical. In 2011, Secretary of State Hillary Clinton announced a proposal for a 'New Silk Road' to drive infrastructure connectivity in Central and West Asia to complement the Obama administration's 'Pivot to Asia'. Both projects were met with much anxiety in Beijing. Chinese officials were upset that America was claiming ownership over the term 'Silk Road', which was otherwise essential to Chinese history. Some Chinese officials, like Shen Weizhong, deputy division director of the department of European Affairs at the Chinese Ministry of Foreign Affairs, were forthright in their assessment that the OBOR was a response to America's pivot to Asia. 'Over the period in which Xi has developed the [OBOR],' he said, '[Xi] has criticized the existing security architecture in Asia, which is built around bilateral security treaties between the US and its allies.'[4] For China, and for Xi especially, the American presence in Asia was anathema to both history and the future balance of powers arrangements. Which is why the OBOR is correctly perceived as a multipurpose vehicle for domestic and regional development and foreign policy. The project is a means to create new markets for China's goods, ease the cost of trading, generate employment and commercial opportunities, improve regional connectivity, and most importantly, restore China's sphere of influence.

RE-MAPPING THE WORLD

Understanding this Chinese project, eventually renamed the Belt and Road Initiative (BRI),[5] requires a deeper appreciation of the megatrends that are shaping the international order and how China's understanding of history and its future ambition fits into them.

The first key observation is that the BRI was China's way of announcing that its time has come. Under Xi, achieving the China Dream required overcoming the most widely documented aspect of its identity, the 'century of humiliation'. In other words, overcoming the humiliation of the Opium Wars of the 1840s, which enfeebled China's otherwise central role in world affairs. As far back as 1959, a US scholar noted that, 'the Chinese have one very broad generalization about their own history: they think in terms of "up to the Opium war" and "after the Opium war".'[6] This is unsurprising, as, in many ways, the Opium Wars bookmarked the decline of both of the major Asian empires, India and China, which were the world's predominant military powers and engines of economic growth until the fifteenth century. Beginning with the maritime voyages of Portugal, Spain, and then England, the world's balance of power shifted decisively in favour of what is now known collectively as the West. Through trade and conquest, European powers would fuel their own industrial revolutions—feeding on raw material and labour from Asian and African colonies. Such was the scale of this empire that by the turn of the twentieth century, Europeans and their colonists ruled 84 per cent of the land and 100 per cent of the sea.[7] Even the period of independence through the mid-twentieth century did little for the former civilizational powers of Asia and Africa, who found themselves dependent on a new order that was crafted to suit the normative and commercial interests of the Atlantic countries. This is not to say that the 'international liberal order', as it is often known, was structurally inimical to the interests of post-colonial societies.

As the post-Cold War era demonstrated, many developing nations rapidly integrated with the global economy, riding on processes, institutions and frameworks that were conceived of by the trans-Atlantic coalition. Nevertheless, they remained absent from the decision-making processes that informed this new order. This 'system' of international engagement, which appealed to many, also allowed the US to emerge as the world's leading economic power in the late-twentieth century. It institutionalized a global human rights agenda, fostered an open trading system through the Bretton Woods institutions, and went on to establish its military presence in Europe, Asia, and the Middle East. Collectively, these were the foundations of Pax Americana—a world order underwritten by American power.

The BRI, more than anything else, marks a decisive turn of events in this long historical trajectory of global political and economic power. In 2014, China became the world's largest economy measured by purchasing power—a first for an Asian power since the fifteenth century, and the first time since 1870 that the US no longer occupied this mantle. If anything, this was simply a culmination of a more significant trend—three of the seven largest economies in the world are now in Asia, China, Japan and India, compared to 1957, when six of the seven largest economies were from Europe and North America. This continuing shift in the balance of global economic power was already the subject of much international scrutiny. In 2012, for example, the US National Intelligence Council (NIC) predicted that by 2030, Asia will have surpassed North America and Europe by every metric of state power, including GDP, military spending and technological investment.[8] Today, China is in a position to capitalize on this tectonic shift, and through the BRI, it is proposing in no uncertain terms that it will shape a new architecture for this power. Many scholars, most notably Singapore's Lee Kuan Yew, have always believed that this was a matter of time. He argued that '[China's] is a culture 4,000 years old with 1.3 billion people, many of great talent... How could they not aspire to be number [one] in Asia, and in time the world?'[9]

The second observation is that China's plan to become number one is quite vague. The BRI's implementation is reminiscent of Deng Xiaoping's 'crossing the river by feeling the stones' approach to economic reforms in the 1970s. By deliberately being short on the specifics, China leaves room for improvisation, course correction, and revision of its intentions and objectives. While Xi's initially vague outlines were more systematically laid out in China's policy document, *Vision and Actions on Jointly Building Silk Road Economic Belt and Twenty-First Century Maritime Silk Road*, Beijing has remained cautious in how it explains the initiative. Even though foreign minister Yi stated that a key focus for Chinese diplomacy was making all-round progress in the BRI, there is no fixed definition of what constitutes this project. While Beijing promises billions in investments, there is little clarity on the number of participating countries, or how China's investments in the BRI differ from its investments in non-BRI countries. A certain tolerance for risk, therefore, is in-built in the design of the BRI. China is willing to invest large sums of money, even though the returns may well be underwhelming, or the possibility that these investments might contribute to financial instability in host countries.

The third observation is that China firmly believes that the Asian continent was split into artificial geographies and that the BRI is capable of rectifying that historical error. As we discussed in the previous chapter, this is an assessment that it shares with India. Like PM Modi, Xi knows that the Asian century will be fundamentally different from the Atlantic century. The region's induction into the new world order was through the process of colonization, leaving very little room for its cultural, philosophical, political, and strategic thought to influence the international system. Most of the sharp divides and divisions between the regions and its communities are a product of European colonialism. This is changing rapidly, and Xi knows this only too well. At a first-of-its-kind Politburo study session on global governance in 2015, Xi hailed the broad geo-strategic trend of Asia's material rise, and the political consequences thereof, as the 'most revolutionary change in the international balance of power since modern times.'[10] The BRI allows China to capitalize on this 'revolutionary change,' by reconnecting the continent.

The countries of the Asian continent are essential to China for three reasons. First, they host secure energy and resource routes from countries in Africa and provide the most direct land routes to Europe. One of the biggest reasons for Chinese overseas investments is to gain access to raw materials and new trade routes. Second, China's investments help buy it political influence in a manner that is detrimental to the interests of other powers in the region. China has used infrastructure loans and investments, for example, to persuade countries like the Philippines and Cambodia to re-evaluate their ties with the US, while its investments in Pakistan help keep India occupied. In time, the BRI will hardwire Chinese influence in Asia. The continent's sprawling network of supply chains will centre on Chinese goods and services, Chinese standards in emerging sectors like 5G and Artificial Intelligence (AI) will become more prominent, and China's currency will be more widely used. Most importantly, Asia will begin to reflect China's preferences for political order and social systems. Increasingly, the Middle Kingdom finds itself well placed to shape the architecture of power that will emerge from Asia. To be clear, however, Asian economies themselves have very little to offer Beijing. For the most part, China's investments in these countries have allowed the Middle Kingdom to create a group of states that are economically dependent on Beijing, while the BRI's ultimate economic purpose is reaching the shores of Europe.

This is the fourth crucial observation. Indeed, the twenty-eight countries that make up the European Union (EU) are currently China's top export market and its prime sources of imports. There are two critical reasons for China's growing political and economic ties with the EU. First, if China is investing in developing countries for raw materials and political influence, much of its overseas investments in high technology supply chains, corporate and business know-how, and brand value has been in one continent: Europe. Consider, for example, that in just one year, between 2015 and 2016, Chinese FDI in Europe increased by around 77 per cent, from £23 billion to £35 billion.[11] This is a concerted effort that is part of China's industrial ambition, especially its attempt to climb the value chain, with both China's twelfth and thirteenth five-year plans encouraging overseas investments in Europe.[12] Additionally, as it moves up the value chain, China views Europe as the only real market for high-end goods. Unsurprisingly, then, China has been investing in key ports across the Mediterranean as a means to create new trade routes into Europe and to gain influence with European states that are at the periphery of the EU.

Second, China seeks to diminish the role of the EU as a global actor even as it engages with its constituent member states to advance its interests. For years, Beijing has promoted the 16+1 diplomatic forum to build its influence with the sixteen Central and Eastern European countries, some of whom belong to the EU or the North Atlantic Treaty Organization (NATO), while others belong to neither. With an economically beleaguered EU unable to provide infrastructure investments at scale, China has stepped into this void to emerge as a European actor. China's investments in Greece's Piraeus port, for example, have helped it become a vital hub of maritime transport in the region. China's motivations, however, are not only economic. Such investments and financial dependencies allow China to divide and rule in the EU. Consider, for example, that in 2017 Greece stopped the EU from criticizing China's human-rights record at a UN forum.[13] Earlier, Greece and Hungary had prevented a joint EU declaration supporting an international tribunal ruling that found China's expansive territorial claims in the South China Sea (SCS) illegal.[14] In essence, Beijing sees a powerful EU bloc as inimical to its political and economic interests in the region and has acted strategically to mitigate the bloc's influence.

China has always believed that the divide between Europe and Asia is an artificial, modern, and particularly Western construct, and it is doing what no other power has had the appetite for: conceive of, define, and then manage a larger Eurasia. In an interdependent global economy, China's global expansion is characterized by a multi-billion-dollar geo-economics thrust capable of creating sprawling networks of connectivity projects, each designed to embed dependency on China's economy into the very geography of the supercontinent. In doing so, China seeks to erode independent regional formulations and identities. This marks another shift in China's foreign policy. From adhering strongly to the principle of 'non-interference' in others' affairs, Beijing now actively uses diplomatic and economic pressure to convince or coerce states to sign on to its geopolitical propositions. Through the BRI, China aims to fundamentally alter the geographies that have defined the twentieth century. Asia and Europe, therefore, are not independent constructs, but part of a Pan-Eurasian system that is reliant on China's network of infrastructure projects. The Middle Kingdom intends to emerge as the sole arbiter of security, development, and economic growth in this supercontinent. China cannot afford to let regionalism distract from this objective, nor can it allow powers like India and collectives like the EU to carve out their own spheres of influence.

REWIRING THE WORLD

This brings us to the final core aspect of understanding the BRI—what does it mean for the international order? Former Australian Prime Minister Kevin Rudd once said, 'Very soon we will find ourselves at a point in history when, for the first time since George III, a non-Western, non-democratic state will be the largest economy in the world. If this is the case,' he speculated, 'how will

China exercise its power in the future international order? Will it accept the culture, norms and structure of the post-war order? Or will China seek to change it?'[15]

In many ways, the BRI provides us with great insight into China's response to this question. It is worth remembering that the initiative itself fits into a broader Chinese ambition, one that is most closely associated with Xi's China Dream. In most official literature, this dream is primarily a domestic one, with the stated goal being for China to achieve 'a moderately prosperous society' by the hundredth anniversary of the Party's founding in 2021, and 'a socialist modernized society' by the hundredth anniversary of the founding of the PRC in 2049. Without a doubt, however, this ambition also has significant implications for the world order. In fact, according to Ye Zicheng, the author of *Inside China's Grand Strategy: The Perspective from the People's Republic*, 'there is a close connection between the "rejuvenation of the Chinese nation"'—a concept very closely associated with Xi—'and China's becoming a world power. If China does not become a world power,' he writes, 'the rejuvenation of the Chinese nation will be incomplete.'[16]

The BRI, then, does much more than bring to mind the varied histories of the Silk Road. Instead, it is a vehicle for China to overcome its 'century of humiliation' and establish its presence as a global power. In other words, the BRI is a long-term roadmap for China's role in the twenty-first century. Despite China's reluctance to appreciate parallels with post-war America, many of its strategies are quite similar, especially at an institutional level. Throughout the twentieth century, the US established several multilateral institutions such as the IMF, the World Bank, and the UN. These institutions would become key to legitimizing America's leadership role in world affairs. Over the first two decades of the twenty-first century, China has built a multilateral framework comparable to Pax Americana, including the AIIB, the Silk Road Fund, the NDB, and several multilateral trade and investment corridors along the BRI region. Like the objectives of American diplomacy, China seeks to create an overarching economic and political network throughout the world, a process that the BRI facilitates. Already, a variety of domestic actors, ranging from provincial governments to national universities to development banks, are part of the BRI in one way or another. At the same time, China has also increasingly centred its bilateral relations around the BRI, not only in terms of economic diplomacy but also through cultural exchange programmes. Through a growing network of commercial and diplomatic ties, China is determining the significance of each state depending on its position within the BRI framework, in which Beijing is at the core of the world's economic system.

As Robert Gilpin writes in his famous work *War and Change in World Politics*, 'states enter social relations and create social structures in order to advance particular sets of political, economic, or other types of interests.'[17] European norms were shaped by centuries of conflict and strife, which ultimately paved the way for the Treaty of Westphalia. Post-1945, the baton of hegemony passed to the US, which successfully propagated the ideals of the Enlightenment and political liberalism through its economic dominance and new international institutions. The norms were ostensibly universal. Human rights and democracy, for example, became deeply embedded in the global system with the adoption of the Universal Declaration of Human Rights by the UN General Assembly (UNGA) in 1948. Free markets and capitalism followed thereafter with the Bretton Woods institutions.

A NEW STATUS QUO

China, like all other great powers, will undoubtedly attempt to influence the international system in a manner that propagates its own ideas, values, norms, and institutions. In a November 2014 speech to the Foreign Affairs Work Conference, the first to be held since 2006, Xi exhorted Chinese officials to develop for China a 'distinctive diplomatic approach befitting its role as a major country,'[18] stressing that China must 'conduct diplomacy with a salient Chinese feature and a Chinese vision.' Earlier in 2013, the Party Committee of the Ministry of Foreign Affairs outlined directives to 'make steady, incremental progress in promoting and guiding the transformation of the international system'[19] based on such principles.

Will China then alter the norms of the international system in tandem with its material rise—thus following a similar trajectory to European and American foreign policy? Or will the international order's comparatively robust architecture constrain China's behaviour sufficiently? Some believe that emerging powers will embrace the international order, underwritten by the globalization of its universal norms and values. John Ikenberry believes that while 'the US' global position may be weakening…the international system the US leads can remain the dominant order of the twenty-first century.'[20] China and other emerging great powers 'do not want to contest the basic rules and principles of the liberal international order; they wish to gain more authority and leadership within.'

However, this has not been true in at least three ways. For one thing, China has bluntly repudiated the role of human rights, both domestically and in the international system. This position is best highlighted by an anecdote about Deng Xiaoping, who once complained to a visiting business delegation that Western talk of 'human rights, freedom, and democracy were designed only to safeguard the interests of the strong, rich countries, which take advantage of their strength to bully weak countries, and which pursue hegemony and practice power politics.'[21] In the 1980s, China's view on human rights positioned it as antagonistic to the liberal aspect of the international order. By 2013, when Document No. 9 explicitly warned against 'Western constitutional democracy' and other 'universal values', China's political choices carried global consequences. Consider, for example, that in 2016, Chinese diplomats were aggressively proposing disinvesting in human rights offices embedded in UN peacekeeping missions and defunding bodies that monitored abuses by UN soldiers to trim the UN's budget.

That same year, the US accused Xi of overseeing a 'deterioration in human rights and rule of law conditions in China marked by greater consolidation of his own power.'[22] Under Chairman Xi, repression at home has become quite routine, along with support for authoritarianism abroad. In Xinjiang, for example, China has built a sprawling surveillance system to suppress the Muslim identity of the local population. In all probability, this is only a precursor of more adverse policy choices at home and around the world.

Second, China has also been gradually altering the rules of commercial conduct, insofar as industry is now a new arm of raw state power. For decades, the Washington Consensus effectively decoupled industry, commerce, and government. China, under Xi, has reversed this trend. In 2010, the *Wall Street Journal* published a front-page story about how the rise of state capitalism was creating a new global economic paradigm. 'Since the end of the Cold War, the world's powers have generally agreed on the wisdom of letting market competition—more than government planning—shape economic outcomes,' the story maintained, warning that, 'China's national economic strategy is disrupting that consensus.'[23]

China is not merely eroding a long-standing consensus on economic growth but is also increasingly employing its state-owned enterprise as tools for its foreign-policy goals. For example, when tensions between China and Japan flared over islands in the East China Sea in 2010, Chinese companies withheld the supply of rare earth minerals to Japan, which are crucial supply chain materials for high-tech industries including cell phones, electric cars, and computer batteries.[24] Unlike Beijing, free-market economies find it more challenging to compel their industrial bodies to take sides on foreign-policy issues. In both matters, i.e., human rights and state capitalism, the BRI is a vehicle for Beijing to alter the international system's normative consensus. Consider, for example, that the UN has warned of 'significant gaps from a human rights perspective' in the funding of the BRI.[25] Unsurprisingly, China is all too happy to fund authoritarian regimes with terrible human rights and governance records, such as Zimbabwe, North Korea, Niger, Angola, and Myanmar. Simultaneously, a report by the Center for Strategic and International Studies (CSIS) notes that of all the contractors involved in the BRI, '89 per cent are Chinese companies, 7.6 per cent are local companies and 3.4 per cent are foreign companies.'[26] This implies that Beijing would have extraordinary leverage to change the norms of corporate governance in countries with weak oversight institutions.

Finally, with respect to adherence to international law as it exists today, China's visibly illegal actions in the SCS raise troubling concerns. Following the Hague tribunal's ruling that all of China's claims under the infamous nine-dash-line were invalid, China responded by calling the decision a 'farce' and one that was 'null and void'.[27] Its state media, on the other hand, merely republished its claims to reaffirm that they were legitimate. China's overbearing relationship with nations in Southeast Asia calls to mind its ancient tributary system, a sprawling network of trade and foreign relations that required smaller states to acknowledge the superiority of China's civilization and kowtow to the emperor. In his widely acclaimed book, *The China Dream*, retired PLA colonel Liu Mingfu states proudly that 'in East Asia's tribute system, China was the superior state, and many of its neighbouring states were vassal states, and they maintained a relationship of tribute and rewards.'[28] It is how China modernizes this ancient conception of order that makes studying its international claim irrelevant, especially because Beijing is unconcerned with whether they possess any legal merit. Instead, the Middle Kingdom's ambivalence about the rules of the international system, along with its historical conceptions of order, suggest that Beijing's ambition is a unipolar Asia. Again, the investments under the BRI only pave the way for China's easy refusal to accept the norms of the international order. Consider, for example, that China's 2017 White Paper on Asia-Pacific Security Cooperation acknowledges that 'security and development are closely linked and mutually complementary,' insofar as one facilitates the other.[29]

The fact is that the prevailing international order tends to reflect contemporary geopolitical realities. As those realities change, the old order must give rise to a new status quo. If, however, we are witnessing a shift in global leadership, the world has no ready template. The last major transition, from Britain to the US, was underpinned by shared religious histories, political values, and institutions. China is undoubtedly the most unlikely sequel to this act. In his book, *The Tragedy of Great Power Politics*, John Mearsheimer once asked why the world expected China's behaviour as a great power to differ from the US'.[30] China's rise, if anything, follows an established pattern of great powers selectively ignoring rules and norms to serve their own interests.

In contrast to Ikenberry's contention that China does not want to challenge the basic rules and premise of the international order, Evan Feigenbaum argues that 'China accepts most forms but not necessarily our preferred norms' of the international system.[31] Indeed, China undoubtedly seeks to work through the framework of established international institutions. However, through the BRI, China aims to rewire the norms and standards of the existing international order to fit more with its image and to extend its economic, political, and normative prescriptions. Through the BRI, Chairman Xi is finally in a position to globalize Chinese ideas of political structures and moral values that are distinct from those born out of the West's enlightenment.

Ultimately, the BRI is a natural extension of many of the overarching foreign policy changes under Xi Jinping, including big ideas such as the China Dream, new policies such as major power diplomacy, and new institutions such as the AIIB. All of this adds to what Xi calls a 'community of common destiny', underpinned by what he calls mutually beneficial cooperation that encompasses 'shared beliefs and norms of conduct for the whole region.' These ideas, as Kevin Rudd persuasively argues, should not be dismissed because Westerners find them 'clunky' or 'meaningless'. Instead, 'this is the language [China] choose[s] to use to communicate' with the world.[32] And as we shall see in the following chapters, the implications these ideas carry for the international order will be far-reaching.

DISTINCT AND ASSERTIVE LEADERSHIP

It is worth also mentioning how vital the BRI is to Chairman Xi's legacy. Bear in mind that the first Chinese official to mention the BRI was Premier Li Keqiang at a China-ASEAN expo in September 2013. As the project grew in scale and ambition, however, Li's mention was soon dropped from official propaganda, and China's state media has fully credited Xi with the initiative. The BRI certainly reflects Xi's distinct and assertive leadership characteristics. It is an enormous undertaking by any metric and showcases a more ambitious and confident Chinese leadership in world affairs.

Since his accession to the presidency, it has become ubiquitous to compare Xi to China's most powerful leader, Mao Zedong. His sweeping crackdown on corruption, and by extension, on political rivals, his absolute control over many of the leading groups that decide key policy, his pervasive control over the extensive propaganda machine that is the China media, and his assertive stance on its territorial disputes bear testament to an immense clout. In October 2016, this personality cult was given an extraordinary boost when Chairman Xi was designated 'core leader' of the Party.[33] In China's political hierarchy, a core leader is one whose teachings, prescriptions, and policies determine China's grand strategy. Only three other Chinese leaders have been anointed core leaders—Mao, Deng Xiaoping and Jiang Zemin—each with their own distinctive legacies. Mao was credited with bringing independence to China, while Deng and Jiang both oversaw the opening up of China's economy, which led to its extraordinary rise. Xi, it appears, is prepared to push further. The BRI is Xi's design for China's re-emergence as a true superpower, one that can proudly bear the mantle of its history.

V

CONTESTED NARRATIVES

The global redistribution of wealth has benefited not just China, but also India—another Asian power with equally strong demographic, political, and economic vectors. For example, the the same 2012 US NIC report which forecasted an Asian tilt in the distribution of global wealth also predicted that by 2030 India could be the 'rising economic powerhouse that China is today.'[1] Apart from China, there are very few emerging countries that seek to achieve a major power status or become a leading power as India has increasingly articulated. While India's economic growth pales in comparison to China's, it has nonetheless been rapid by all measures. After India launched an expansive set of economic reforms, its GDP grew tenfold, from $274 billion in 1991 to just over $2 trillion in 2015.[2] Present-day studies suggest that by the middle of the century, India will be the second-largest economic power measured by purchasing power parity (PPP). In many ways, this rise was supported by the international order under Pax Americana, but the process was not without friction. New Delhi benefited from global capital flows through the turn of the twenty-first century, a mostly benign external security environment, and global governance institutions that were slowly accommodating its rise.

However, China's newfound ambition under Xi has threatened this equilibrium. As Beijing's influence begins to grow, India's interests in this emerging geopolitical gambit will be contested. This explains why China was keen to have India on board with the BRI. The Middle Kingdom could hardly afford to breed insecurity in an emerging Asian power like India. Instances of past cooperation, such as on the NDB and the AIIB, have provided the foundation for India-China cooperation in the sphere of multilateral finance and development. More importantly, many of the belts and roads in China's initial design would pass through India, due to its location at the intersection of continental Asia and the Indian Ocean Region (IOR). Both countries have long cooperated on the Bangladesh-China-India-Myanmar (BCIM) economic corridor—a network of road, air and waterways that would link Kolkata to Kunming in southeast China. In fact, in late 2014, Xi claimed that China would 'discuss the initiatives of the Silk Road Economic Belt and the Twenty-first Century Maritime Silk Road' with India.[3] In a 2015 interview with *The Hindu*, then Chinese ambassador to India, Le Yucheng, claimed that India was China's 'natural and significant partner' in promoting the BRI initiatives, citing that India's participation in the AIIB was an example of how both countries could cooperate.[4]

HARD REALITIES

Sitting in New Delhi, however, one was struck by three realities of China's Belt and Road that made such an]accommodation difficult, if not impossible. The first, of course, was sovereignty. As early as 2013, Premier Keqiang visited Pakistan and announced a new economic corridor that would connect China's Kashgar region with Pakistan's Gwadar Port. Gwadar is a strategic piece of infrastructure that sits across the Strait of Hormuz and sees nearly a third of the world's oil trade pass by it. There was, of course, a catch: the planned infrastructure project would pass through Gilgit–Baltistan, a territory long disputed between Pakistan and India and claimed by both. While this caused much anxiety in India at the time, Delhi continued to maintain a neutral stance on the BRI, choosing to hash out the issue with China instead. Speaking to reporters after a round of strategic dialogue between India and China on 14 April 2014, then Indian foreign secretary Sujatha Singh confirmed that India had raised the matter with China.[5]

By the time Modi decided to visit China in 2015, the tone and tenure of India's approach to the BRI was changing. It was increasingly apparent that the project was not designed to offer any opportunities to India or other powers in the region. Former foreign secretary Shivshankar Menon once made this point when he argued that foreign countries would benefit from the BRI 'to the extent that non-Chinese firms can compete and participate in creating local and regional production networks.'[6] Unfortunately, the BRI has followed another path Menon had outlined, one where 'there is an attempt to push a political agenda, exclud[e] economic rivals, [and] pursu[e] political or security goals.' This is the second reality that one has to take into consideration; not only was the BRI violating Indian sovereignty, but it was also cutting India out of regional connectivity initiatives and economic partnerships. Replying to questions from journalists ahead of the Modi-Xi meeting, then foreign secretary Jaishankar bluntly stated that the Silk Road was 'China's initiative'. To the best of India's knowledge, he added, Beijing had 'not really had a detailed discussion on this subject.'[7] It did not help that a month ahead of Modi's visit to China, Xi was in Pakistan reaffirming the $46 billion investment in the 2000-mile infrastructure and a connectivity push across the country. Modi himself is said to have raised the issue of the China-Pakistan Economic Corridor (CPEC) very strongly during his visit to Beijing, reportedly conveying to his counterparts that this state of affairs was unacceptable.[8] As China pressed on with the BRI, however, showing little intention to engage with India, New Delhi became more public with its reservations and concerns. Jaishankar fired the opening salvo in this act in 2015 and his comments deserve reproduction in full: 'Where we are concerned, this is a national Chinese initiative. The Chinese devised it, created a blueprint. It wasn't an international initiative they discussed with the world, with countries that are interested or affected by it… A national initiative is devised with national interests, it is not incumbent on others to buy it.'[9]

It is worth pointing out that India and China have cooperated on multilateral economic and developmental initiatives before. We don't need to look any further than the AIIB, an institution that India supported and benefits from. Indeed, the Sino-Indian relationship has always been characterized by sidelining political disagreements even as they cooperated elsewhere. It was clear to India, however, that the BRI was a fundamentally different proposition. If the CPEC was emblematic of China's failure to consult India on consequential connectivity projects, the following months only heightened anxiety in India over the motivations behind the project. Increasingly, it was apparent to New Delhi that connectivity was merely a tool to expand Beijing's influence in the region in a manner that would be detrimental to India's interests and regional balance of power arrangements. Mahinda Rajapaksa, for example, had awarded several infrastructure projects to Chinese companies and accepted loans that amounted to nearly $4 billion by the end of 2014.[10] More worryingly, his presidency also coincided with the first visit of a People's Liberation Army Navy (PLAN) submarine to Colombo, a significant security concern for New Delhi. Even after Maithripala Sirisena defeated Rajapaksa in the 2015 elections, his government's investigation into the terms of these loans raised strong suspicions that China was willing to purchase influence in Asia through the BRI. By this time, many pundits were beginning to question the true motivations of China's investments—especially considering that the economics behind the project was slowly unravelling. According to Oxford's Saïd Business School, nearly 55 per cent of the projects that China had invested in were economically unviable at the outset, and another 17 per cent generated lower-than-forecasted benefit-to-cost ratio. The report concluded that only 28 per cent of such projects could be considered financially viable.[11]

More importantly, China's investments had started to take on a more strategic edge and the industrial hubs that Beijing had planned to develop were also capable of enabling military operations. In 2014, the PLAN's Naval Research Institute recommended that China build replenishment and logistics points at key ports to better protect its energy supply lines.[12] According to the report, the Kyaukpyu Port in Myanmar, the Chittagong Port in Bangladesh, the Colombo Harbour in Sri Lanka, the Aden Port in Yemen, and ports in the Maldives were potential locations where the Chinese government could work to create industrial hubs to support military operations. Bear in mind that these designs show an uncomfortable resemblance to China's 'string of pearls' strategy, which would encircle India and reduce its room to manoeuvre in the IOR. Chinese scholars enthusiastically suggested that Beijing follow a 'civilian first, then military' strategy for many of its infrastructure projects. Under this principle, commercial infrastructure would be built to eventually develop them into strategic support points that would assist China in projecting maritime power.

Such thinking prompted another reassessment of the BRI by India. In 2015, former foreign secretary Shyam Saran observed that China was carving out a separate 'continental-maritime realm' for itself in Asia that would consign India to a Chinese-led Asian order.[13] This was the third reality of the BRI for India. Through its economic investments, Beijing was willing and able to forcefully alter both the geography of Asia as well as its normative framework. Unsurprisingly, the Indian view on the BRI was no longer one of indifference, but of increasing concern. As Jaishankar commented more substantively at India's flagship conference on geopolitics, the Raisina Dialogue, in March 2016, 'The interactive dynamic between strategic interests and connectivity initiatives an exercise in hardwiring influence.'[14] The argument that the BRI could create perverse dependencies was not far-fetched. Consider, for example, that less than two weeks after the citizens of Philippines elected Rodrigo Duterte as president in June 2016, the Hague tribunal ruled in favour of the country's maritime claims in the SCS, which China had steadily militarized over the past few years. Instead of piling the pressure on Xi, Duterte engineered an unlikely entente with China, pivoting away from long-time ally the US and going so far as to call President Obama a 'son of a bitch' and telling him to 'go to hell'.[15] Unsurprisingly, the seventy-one-year-old populist visited Beijing later in October and secured infrastructure deals worth $13 billion.[16] As it turns out, the ASEAN community as a whole was unable to adopt a joint resolution condemning China's blatant violation of international law in the SCS following the Hague verdict—an ambiguity for which many leaders in the region were richly rewarded. Malaysian Prime Minister Najib Razak, for example, visited China in November that year, returning with about $34 billion worth of deals.[17] Renmin University scholar Pang Zhongying argued that China was better placed to develop ties with its neighbours through the ancient strategy of 'Huairou' or mollification through financial inducements; in other words, 'pacifying and winning the hearts of foreigners through tributary trade.'[18]

Beijing was certainly pacifying foreign leaders, whether it was through winning their hearts or buying them out. India was made bluntly aware of this reality when Sri Lankan Prime Minister Sirisena capitulated to China over the Hambantota Port. Despite his overt preference for India, Sirisena was handicapped by what is now a regular feature of China's investments—massive debt obligations of the receipt country. Of the nearly $5 billion worth of loans China advanced between 2005 and 2012 to Sri Lanka, only 2 per cent took the form of outright grants. The rest were loans at commercial interest rates. This took a toll on Sri Lanka's foreign debt, which bloated to 94 per cent of its GDP by 2015.[19] In a perverse arrangement to service this debt, Sri Lanka was forced to hand over the Hambantota Port to China on a ninety-nine-year-long lease. A similar situation has played out in the Maldives, with former President Nasheed claiming that the country owes nearly $3.5 billion to various Chinese contractors and banks.[20]

Like with states in the Indian Ocean and the Pacific Ocean, these dynamics were also playing out in continental Asia, where the landlocked Central Asian nations were heavily indebted to China. The Export-Import Bank (Exim Bank) of China, for example, holds nearly 41 per cent and 53 per cent of all government debt in Kyrgyzstan and Tajikistan, respectively.[21] Just like in Sri Lanka, China's investments were increasingly directed towards securing strategic infrastructure or raw materials, with nearly a third of all Chinese investments in Central Asia going into the energy sector alone. In this region as well, China's investments were interfering with local political processes. In 2016, for example, Kyrgyz Prime Minister Temir Sariyev was forced to resign following long-drawn- out protests over his association with Chinese enterprise. A parliamentary commission report accused him of illicitly awarding nearly $100 million worth of infrastructure contracts to Chinese firms.[22]

A NEW LOW IN BILATERAL RELATIONS

For India, the tensions with China over the means and methods of Asian connectivity were only exacerbated by the fact that the broader Sino-India relationship was hitting new lows by 2016. China had refused to support a UN resolution that would have declared the Pakistan-based Jaish-e-Mohammed (JeM) chief Masood Azhar an international terrorist. Later, it refused to support India's bid for the Nuclear Suppliers Group (NSG). Also, Beijing seemed entirely unresponsive to India's growing concern over its trade deficit, which at the time was a little over $60 billion. China's almost clumsy and unilateral approach with India over the BRI only added to these frustrations. It did not help that China had otherwise gone to great lengths to pacify other countries. With Russia, China was keen to demonstrate how the BRI would reinforce Moscow's economic integration plans in Eurasia. But Beijing made no such efforts with India, and even went so far as to include Indian ports in quasi-official maps of the BRI. The BCIM corridor, for example, was written into the scheme even though India had made no such agreement.[23] Worryingly for India, it appeared that other nations, including the major powers, were almost too eager to join the BRI. Germany's Chancellor Angela Merkel, for example, was enthusiastic about the BRI's potential to catalyse investments in Europe.[24] Mixed signals were emerging from the US, Australia, and Japan as well, with many keen on capitalizing on the economic opportunities of the initiative. In a diplomatic blow to India, even the United Nations Security Council (UNSC) endorsed the BRI, in the context of improving regional development in Afghanistan, despite India's evident opposition to the CPEC.[25]

By May 2017, a critical choice presented itself to Indian policymakers. On 14 May, Xi welcomed leaders from nearly twenty-eight countries, delegates from over one hundred countries, along with leaders from key international institutions to the Belt and Road Forum in Beijing. The first of its kind, the Forum was a massive two-day event to officially highlight China's position as the centre of a new economic order. Again, China was only too keen to bring India on board, dispatching dozens of invites to top ceremonial and political offices, including several current ministers, diplomats, and former envoys, besides other scholars and journalists. A week ahead of the Forum, Chinese ambassador to India, Luo Zhaohui, even offered to rename the CPEC, ostensibly to allay Indian concerns that China was taking a diplomatic stance over the question of Kashmir, although China's official press release erased any mention of this offer the very next day.[26] For New Delhi, however, scepticism towards the BRI was now about more than sovereignty. India was never a bit player in Asia and its role in this vital geography was being heavily implicated by the BRI. It was increasingly apparent to India that a failure to respond to China's proposition could well allow China to shape Asia unilaterally.

A day before the BRI forum, the consensus in New Delhi was clear—the BRI offered India no economic opportunity, nor did it attempt to include India in its design. Therefore, it was certain that India would not send any representative to the event. For a country that had rarely chosen confrontational policy options towards Beijing, it undoubtedly surprised observers that India was reserving support for the BRI. More importantly, even as countries like the US and Japan were privately hedging their options, India emerged as a lone critic of the project, stating in unequivocal terms that 'connectivity initiatives must be based on universally recognized international norms, good governance, the rule of law, openness, transparency and equality.'[27]

Despite India's absence, it is worth pointing out that the Forum was a success by almost any metric. Surrounded by dozens of world leaders in a carefully choreographed event, Xi called the BRI 'the project of the century', projecting China as a global economic powerhouse and a leading advocate of free trade.[28] Historians were hard-pressed to miss the symbolism of world leaders stepping up to shake hands with Chairman Xi—a twenty-first-century vision of the Middle Kingdom's ancient tributary system. The media frenzy during and after the event not only succeeded in cementing China's emergence as a global leader but also burnished Xi's credentials ahead of the critical nineteenth Party Congress later that year.

The success of the Belt and Road Forum did not impress India, to whom it was apparent that the BRI served only one actor—Beijing. The sixty-odd nations that have signed up for the BRI are relatively small and in dire need of infrastructure finance, and China's loose purse strings are an attractive option. However, these countries have neither the agency nor the capacity to guard against China's predatory economic practices or its political influence. Through debt, political influence, and outright coercion, the BRI is a roadmap for structural servility to Beijing. The fact remains that leading powers like India, with the political will and the economic and military agency to shape the Asian order, cannot accept this option. From New Delhi's perspective, many of its neighbours are straddled with immense debt, and by extension, political subservience to Beijing. This leads to a situation where China is unilaterally scripting the security architecture in Asia. For a country that has always preferred multipolarity and multilateralism, both globally and regionally, acquiescing to Pax Sinica was never truly an option.

DOKLAM STANDOFF: PRECURSOR TO A SINO-INDIAN COLD WAR

Failing to acquiesce to China's ambitions, however, can often have adverse consequences. Less than a month after India's refusal to bandwagon on to Beijing's BRI, Delhi found itself in an eyeball-to-eyeball military standoff with China on the Doklam Plateau, an 89-square-mile territory that sits at the junction of the India-China-Bhutan border in the Himalayas. This was a standoff between two of Asia's largest powers, each with its own history and increasingly divergent vision for the region. It took place at a time when economic and strategic trends were propelling Asia to the centre of global politics. It is unsurprising, therefore, that one of the most dangerous escalations in Sino-Indian conflict in nearly five decades should come at this time. While this dispute was contained at the border, the Doklam standoff is better understood as the first skirmish for leadership and national space between the two Himalayan giants for the future of the Asian century. Indeed, should India and China fail to manage the many disagreements that are now appearing in their relationship, historians may well remember the Doklam standoff as the precursor to a Sino-Indian Cold War.

To understand this conflict, it is best to start at the beginning. A PLA construction party began working on infrastructure development in the area sometime around 16 June 2017. Bhutan, which claims the region, attempted to dissuade Chinese troops from continuing any further, conveying to China that its construction activities violated several agreements that required both countries to maintain the status quo pending a final settlement of the border alignment. Soon after, India, which is party to a 'Treaty of Friendship' with Bhutan that empowers it to guide the country's foreign policy,[29] sent troops to block Chinese construction activities physically. On 30 June, India released an official statement on the matter, making it clear that China's actions on the plateau 'would represent a significant change of status quo with security implications for India.'[30]

For New Delhi, China's activities were taking place uncomfortably close to the Siliguri corridor, a narrow stretch of land connecting mainland India to its Northeastern states. Allowing China to maintain a presence at Doklam would ease Beijing's access to the Jampheri ridge, a critical high ground that could disrupt Indian activities in Siliguri. China, on the other hand, continued to maintain its physical presence, arguing from the beginning that the territory belonged to Beijing. As early as 26 June, Geng Shuang, China's foreign ministry spokesperson, criticized India's intervention. China's position was that Indian troops 'crossed the China-India boundary at the Sikkim section and entered the Chinese territory, obstructing Chinese border troops' normal activities in Doklam.'[31] Unlike several such confrontations in the past, however, Beijing decided to up the rhetoric this time around. On 5 July, China's ambassador to India, Luo Zhaohui, claimed that there was no scope for compromise until India entirely withdrew its troops from the region—a position that was decidedly untenable for India.[32]

Boundary disputes are not new to either nation. China and India share an undefined and unsettled border that is approximately 3,500 kilometres long and even fought a brief war in 1962. Thus, the de facto border, otherwise known as the Line of Actual Control (LAC), has witnessed numerous confrontations and standoffs between Indian and Chinese patrols. While the situation is analogous to the more fiercely contested India-Pakistan border, several bilateral processes between China and India have ensured that this border has been free of any fatal confrontations.

The Doklam standoff, however, was different in many ways. Firstly, it took place on the soil of a third party—Bhutan. Secondly, nationalism had become a defining mood in politics under both Modi and Xi. The fact that the same territory had witnessed heavy military clashes between the two countries in 1967 added to the already tense sentiments prevailing in India and China. Furthermore, Xi was preparing for China's Nineteenth Party Congress later that August, a bi-decennial event that celebrates China's leadership and a platform where Xi could hardly afford to lose face. Thirdly, at a time when both Asian powers were staking a claim to leadership in the region, India and China had increasingly found themselves pitted against each other in regional and global affairs. At the local level, India had stepped up construction of military infrastructure along the border, while deepening economic and security cooperation with several Asian partners, alongside the US. For China, an Asian region with a robust Indian presence limits its ability to act unilaterally, and it had strong incentives to keep India from believing that its influence was on par with Beijing's. Not only did the standoff take place soon after India's vocal opposition to the BRI, but it was also made public on 26 June, just as Modi was slated to visit President Trump in Washington. One can hypothesize that China wanted to remind India of the costs that Beijing could impose on India in response to a pro-US or overtly anti-China tilt.

A CONTEST FOR THE FUTURE OF ASIA

There are two key facets of the Doklam standoff that are worth studying. The first, of course, is the military dynamics. For observers around the world, China's Doklam gambit had many features in common with its militarization of the SCS. As Oriana Skylar Mastro and Arzan Tarapore have pointed out, China's 'coercion playbook' ordinarily involves four elements.[33] First, 'develop a large or permanent physical presence.' Second, aggressive diplomacy through repeated threats of military action. Third, lawfare, which involves advancing legal claims to justify its military aggression. And finally, an offensive media blitzkrieg. At Doklam, all four were on display. Less than a month after China's incursion became public, 7,000 PLA troops conducted large-scale, live-fire exercises near Arunachal Pradesh.[34] The fact that China's economy was roughly five times larger than India's only added to Beijing's foreboding presence. This was followed by aggressive rhetoric from official Chinese sources, warning India's that its troops 'faced three options at Doklam as the standoff entered one month: withdrawal, capture or an attack by China, should the dispute escalate.'[35] China's Deputy Director-General of the Boundary and Ocean Affairs also threatened to expand the scope of the standoff, warning India that China could also 'enter the Kalapani region between China, India and Nepal or even into the Kashmir region between India and Pakistan.'[36] China's nationalist *Global Times* rabidly published scathing op-eds threatening that Beijing may support 'pro-independence appeal[s] in Sikkim' and that 'India will suffer worse losses than 1962 if it incites border clashes'.[37] All of this was buttressed by China's claims that an 1890 treaty between China and the erstwhile British Empire cemented its legal claim. China made this claim even though multiple rounds of dialogue and legal agreements between India, China, and Bhutan established that the border dispute would be settled through consultation rather than unilateral action. China almost always follows this multipronged approach: creating uncertainty about its intention, threatening existential costs for conflict, and controlling the media narrative by painting itself as a victim. Bit by bit, China has used these tactics to advance its revisionist claims in the SCS and was now bringing them to the Himalayas.

The second factor in this dispute was diplomacy and the quest for regional influence. The standoff was a crucial test of India's willingness to stand up for Bhutan and, by extension, its resolve to participate in shaping the future of the Asian century. Writing for the *South China Morning Post*, John Glover argued that the Doklam standoff was China's way of telling India to 'accept changing realities'.[38] In other words, New Delhi had to acquiesce to China's overbearing presence in South Asia as an extension of its bid for Asian hegemony. Thus, China had strong imperatives to woo Bhutan as a diplomatic partner, by force or otherwise. India and Bhutan have maintained a special relationship since 1949, which allowed Delhi to exercise a considerable veto over the Himalayan kingdom's foreign policy. And while this treaty was amended in 2007 to grant Bhutan greater autonomy, Delhi continues to enjoy some sway over the kingdom. Bhutan also happens to be the only South Asian country that has not established official diplomatic relations with Beijing, and also the only country to join India's boycott of the BRI. This not only creates a physical barrier for China's attempts to reconnect the Asian continent but also hurts its image as the region's pre-eminent power. Which is why Beijing chose to paint India's response at Doklam as a neo-colonial gambit, claiming that Delhi's incursion violated both Chinese and Bhutanese sovereignty.[39] At the same time, Beijing was dangling very attractive financial inducements, reportedly offering a $10 billion assistance package of grants, direct investment and low-interest loans to the landlocked Bhutanese kingdom.[40]

This story was consistent with China's rising influence in India's neighbourhood. Nepal, for example, eagerly signed on to the BRI in a bid to reduce its dependence on Indian trade and security. Myanmar, similarly, was developing Kyaukpyu in the Bay of Bengal region with nearly $10 billion in Chinese funding.[41] Bangladesh, meanwhile, was emerging as a key market for Chinese arms and defence products and had attracted almost $25 billion in Chinese investments.[42] In Sri Lanka, as we have already seen, Maithripala Sirisena was unable to resist the financial implications of the Hambantota port, inevitably leasing the port to China for ninety-nine years. Similarly, in the Maldives, China had acquired an uninhabited island near Male on a fifty-year lease at the cost of $4 million.[43] Like elsewhere in the region, Beijing's carrot-and-stick approach with Bhutan sought to convince the kingdom that India could not guarantee its security interests if it angered Beijing, while simultaneously making it clear that setting up diplomatic relations with Beijing would bring it untold benefits. At the same time, China was establishing that its presence was now a permanent feature not just in East Asia, but also in South Asia, which was otherwise considered India's strategic sphere of influence.

The broader stakes in the conflict were quite clearly around leadership in Asia. That is why India's response at the time elicited much attention. New Delhi was quick to mobilize a physical response at Doklam—effectively thwarting Beijing's attempt to seize territory. Analysts have often juxtaposed this firm response to failed deterrence strategies in Southeast Asia with regard to China's militarization in the SCS, where the Middle Kingdom perfected its salami-slicing tactics. The 2012 Scarborough Shoal incident, where China claimed control of the Philippines's legitimate economic zone under the pretext of protecting traditional fishing grounds is a common analogy.[44] Following a short standoff in the region, the Philippines government withdrew military vessels from the area, leaving China with control over what it calls the Huang Yan islands. At Doklam, however, China was effectively presented with a fait accompli. It undoubtedly helped India that it maintained a local military advantage. As commentator Ajay Shukla points out, this region was 'where India attacks China, not the other way around.'[45] Additionally, compared to China, India's response was more measured, with politicians and the media generally refraining from irresponsible rhetoric. India's desired end goal was also clear: for both countries to respect the status quo as it was before the standoff began. Then foreign secretary Jaishankar maintained throughout the confrontation that India's diplomatic channels were open and that India saw no reason that the dispute could not be resolved through dialogue.[46] Even India's otherwise vocal

Opposition parties maintained a firm commitment to protecting India's interests in the region, refusing to play domestic politics over the standoff. At the same time, Delhi continually kept Thimphu apprised of the situation through backdoor channels, ensuring that the Himalayan kingdom did not consider faltering on its claims.

While the prolonged standoff did send jitters across the continent, Delhi's firm response was being studied with great interest by the Southeast Asian countries who were keen on co-opting India to balance China's rise. The same was true for other countries around the world. By August, both Japan and the US had issued statements asking Delhi and Beijing to restore the status-quo, which were signs of implicit support for India's position.[47] New Delhi also benefited from a bit of luck as China was pegged to host the ninth BRICS summit in Xiamen that year. While the events on Doklam continued to remain tense, New Delhi sent strong signals that Prime Minister Modi would not attend, a fact that would reflect negatively on China's global leadership claims and cause much embarrassment to Xi.[48]

By 28 August, it had become clear that affairs at Doklam were at an impasse—neither side wanted a military confrontation, while the negative diplomatic and political externalities of a prolonged standoff were irrational for both countries. Hence, both countries ultimately chose to disengage on the plateau, leading to a solution that was India's desired goal. For China, the experience at Doklam was a sobering lesson on New Delhi's conceptions of being a major power in Asia and its ability and willingness to act decisively when national-security interests were involved. On a tactical level, China failed to put India in its place following Delhi's public and vocal opposition to the BRI. At the regional level, Beijing was unable to induce Bhutan into voicing disagreement with India. Therefore, for China, the Doklam standoff was a clear illustration that it would have to take higher risks and expend significant resources if it wanted to teach India a lesson.

India's willingness to confront China was quite a unique

moment. For the past few years, China has successfully employed its coercion playbook to thwart competitors in the SCS, including the US. No other state has intervened on behalf of a third party to guard against China's interventionism. Nevertheless, it is incorrect to paint this episode as an Indian 'win'—as many commentaries suggested at the time. For one thing, Beijing never did entirely withdraw. The Chinese foreign ministry, for its part, indicated that 'Indian forces have already withdrawn to the Indian side of the border,' implying that Delhi withdrew first, and that 'Chinese forces will continue to patrol in [the] Doklam region…to exercise [China's] sovereignty over the region.'[49] China has continued its revisionism and diplomatic hand-wrangling with Bhutan, along with similar expansionism in most of India's neighbourhood. In addition, as Taylor Fravel convincingly argues, India's actions at Doklam did not truly present a 'model' for preventing China's territorial grab in the SCS or elsewhere—nor might it be easily replicable by New Delhi in the future.[50] In 2017, India was fortunate to enjoy a local tactical advantage, unlike many of the claimants in the SCS. Furthermore, India's intervention in Bhutan had some legal sanction under the shared defence arrangement. The US, on the other hand—the only other major power in Southeast Asia—was officially a 'neutral' third party and could not actively intervene to protect claims. Thus, the picture that emerges from Doklam is one of complexity. It was clear that the dispute raised larger questions of Asian leadership and of regional security, and more broadly, it set the tone for an emerging power competition between India and China.

Even as China is intent on shaping an order that will be dictated by the Middle Kingdom, New Delhi is asserting its own governance preferences. The India-China relationship is therefore coming to signify a contest for the future of Asia, as well as the world at large. At issue is whether nation-states that exercised their hard-won right to self-determination and democracy will now be forced into a client-satellite relationship with Beijing, especially as its economic dominance continues. Over the past seven decades, the international liberal order was carefully crafted to promote free markets, the rule of law, and democracy. Leadership with Chinese characteristics, discernible most visibly through the BRI, offers a counter proposition to these norms and rules.

For India, on the other hand, the Doklam standoff may well have catalysed new thinking about its role in the international order. India can no longer afford to merely be a stakeholder in this order. Instead, it will need to defend and support it proactively. Undermining India may have been China's greatest miscalculation yet. By alienating another rising power, Beijing is all but guaranteeing that policies that are antagonistic to China will accompany India's rise. In the final analysis, if the officials in New Delhi and Beijing have learnt the right lessons from Doklam, we may still see the political and material rise of Asia play out peacefully. On the other hand, if the two Asian giants continue to pursue their different postures, Doklam will come to be remembered as the beginning of a great new game in Asia, with potentially fatal consequences.

VI

INDIA'S SPACE TO MANOEUVRE

While the Doklam standoff represents the height of tensions between the two Asian powers in the Himalayas, it would be amiss to ignore their contest in the Indian Ocean and South Asia more broadly. If Asia is ground zero for the leadership of the Asian century, South Asia and its waters are where the implications of these political dynamics will be felt the earliest. Developments in the Maldives towards the end of 2018 are a useful starting point for deconstructing the India-China relationship in this region. Observers of Asian politics will remember that PM Modi's visit to Male in November 2018 was preceded by a series of dramatic events in the island state, which ended with the ouster of President Abdulla Yameen, who had imposed a state of emergency earlier in January.[1] The restoration of democratic rule in the archipelago and the positive overtures towards India from the new government of President Ibrahim Mohamed Solih were widely perceived as a vindication of India's neighbourhood policy. It is easy to see why the Indian commentariat was pleased with the results. The year 2018 was tough for India's regional leadership ambitions, and events in the Maldives had made abundantly clear the velocity with which China's raw economic power was overwhelming India's long-standing civilizational influence in the region.

It is worth remembering that until 2012, Beijing didn't even have an embassy in the Maldives. The announcement of the BRI, however, prompted a diplomatic course correction. Having already invested nearly $21.5 billion in Bangladesh to develop port infrastructure, over $62 billion on the CPEC to make the the Gwadar port accessible to Chinese trade and security interests, and a first overseas military base in Djibouti, the Maldives was a natural investment to make. Setting aside major trade and energy routes that flow from the Gulf of Aden to the Strait of Malacca, the Maldives is situated at a strategically important location. A strong Chinese presence in Male would allow Beijing to secure its increasing global interests while also placing India in a vulnerable position. The fact that it was a small economy with unfulfilled development needs also fit perfectly into China's playbook. By 2018, China was responsible for significant infrastructure development projects in the country, including an $800-million airport and a $400-million bridge to connect it with the capital city, Male.[2] A Free Trade Agreement (FTA), signed amidst much controversy about its opacity, leased Maldivian islands to China for redevelopment and tourism for fifty years.[3] At the same time, India's strategic and commercial interests were gradually sidelined, much to the displeasure of New Delhi, which was increasingly uncertain about how to manage China's rise in its neighbourhood.

This pattern of Chinese and Indian hostile interaction in regional governance was inevitable. As early as 1991, India launched its Look East policy in tandem with embracing the international economic order. While the quest for new commercial and energy opportunities were India's main priorities, 'strategic interests' vis-à-vis China also figured in Delhi's calculus. Given that much of China's trade and energy flows through maritime South Asia, Beijing has always 'acted' west to maintain a weaker Indian presence. For instance, in 1993, General Zhao Nanqi, then director of the Chinese

Academy of Military Sciences, warned that China was 'not prepared to let the Indian Ocean become India's Ocean'.[4] That one region should host two rising competitive powers makes the study of South Asia so important. As Shyam Saran correctly observed in 2006, it is in Asia 'where the interests of both India and China intersect...the logic of geography is unrelenting.'[5] Their pattern of interactions in South Asia reveals the contours of an emerging contest for primacy in the twenty-first century.

DECONSTRUCTING CHINA'S SOUTH ASIA

While many in India celebrated the events in the Maldives as a pro-India diplomatic victory, such euphoria may have been premature. The turnaround in Male was prompted more by domestic political compulsions than by Indian or Chinese machinations. New Delhi must not forget lessons from Sri Lanka, where Rajapaksa's ouster did little to limit China's influence. This only underlines the fact that China is a permanent actor in South Asian politics, and that most of India's neighbours have cozied up to Beijing in one way or another.

Still, New Delhi is searching, and sometimes struggling, for space to manoeuvre in its own subcontinent. As New Delhi attempts to recalibrate its imperfect relationship with its neighbours, it would do well to carefully examine the realities that have allowed China to 'win' against India in a series of diplomatic encounters in South Asia. For one thing, the most important economic actor in South Asia today is Beijing. In a region that faces an annual $2.5 trillion infrastructure finance shortfall and one that is the least integrated with the world,[6] China alone has invested nearly $150 billion in the last decade, and much more is promised under the BRI.[7] With a clear agenda for economic integration and no antecedents of military interventions in the region, China remains a welcome partner for most South Asian states.

To the detriment of Delhi's economic and security interests,

India's failure to emerge as an economic locomotive for the region, coupled with its troubled history in its neighbourhood, has only enhanced China's appeal. Nepal has recently reminded India of this by granting development rights for the $2.5-billion Budhi Gandaki hydropower project to China, even after the previous government cancelled it.[8] It also participated in the second joint military exercise with China in September 2018.[9] Beijing has leveraged the fact that most of India's smaller neighbours bear some resentment or the other against India's behaviour in the region. Indeed, reporting from China's state media tirelessly paints India in hegemonic colours in South Asia, seeking to strengthen the negative perception of India.

China has also benefited from a democratic deficit in the region while India's desire for liberalism to take root in the region never materialized. In the Maldives, President Yameen had exercised unlawful powers to arrest and jail political opponents and curb free speech. Meanwhile identity politics and nationalism were buffeting India's neighbourhood in general. In this climate, China's experiences in Southeast Asia informed its behaviour towards South Asian states. In December 2017, for example, China voted against a UN resolution that condemned Myanmar's crackdown on the Rohingya and continued to invest billions in the crisis-hit Rakhine state.[10] Its relationship with Cambodia's Hun Sen and with Duterte in the Philippines is much the same. China funnelled over $800 million into controversial dam projects in Cambodia[11] and praised Duterte's 'remarkable achievement' in protecting human rights even as his violent anti-drug campaign unfolded. Countries like Pakistan, where democratic institutions are mostly dysfunctional, have essentially become client states to Beijing. Even though India is hardly evangelical about democracy promotion, it will nonetheless find navigating these trends difficult, especially as it overtly associates with democracies like the US, Japan, and Australia.

As in other regions, Beijing has employed a successful multifaceted toolkit for building relationships with smaller states in South Asia, while preventing larger ones from securing their regional arrangements. This toolkit includes: first, a massive credit-fuelled investment in the region. Second, consolidating relationships with political elites or business leaders and exploiting them for political leverage. For instance, Beijing invested questionably in Rajapaksa's constituencies when he was president of Sri Lanka. Third, heightened political interference. Following significant investments from China, Hungary and Greece, for example, refused to support an EU statement on the SCS. Fourth, building or interfering in regional institutions—whether it is the in Central Asia, a new China-South Asia Cooperation Forum (which will operate parallel to the SAARC process), or its divide and rule approach with the ASEAN. Finally, tactical military interventions against incumbent powers, as we have seen in Doklam and in China's militarization of the South China Sea.

Caught between these two realities, South Asian states have acted quite predictably by hedging their bets between Delhi and Beijing. Long dependent on India for investment and security, they have naturally courted China to meet their development needs and enhance their bargaining power with Delhi. This has worked for them. Even as India's neighbours accept investments under the BRI, they have emerged as the primary destinations for Indian investment and aid. In the past year alone, for example, India provided a $4.5 billion line of credit to Bangladesh,[12] invested $2 billion in Sri Lanka to upgrade port and other infrastructure facilities,[13] and announced new cross-border rail and waterway connectivity projects with Nepal.

As Beijing continues to pursue its project of connecting Asia, Africa, and Europe, it seeks to erode South Asia's potential as an independent regional formulation and India's ability to retain its sphere of influence. Rather than investing in organic regional processes, China conscripts smaller states into aligning their infrastructure and trade policies with its Belt and Road network. This allows China to find commercial opportunity in the global value chains that the BRI is creating while reducing dependence on Indian investment and markets. For China, a distinct South Asian identity is purposeless. Instead, a handful of strategic client states like Pakistan and a system of economic patronage with countries like Bangladesh, Nepal, and Sri Lanka serve the security and commercial interests of its global ambition. The entire South Asian sub-region is only a single working part of China's broader Eurasian objective. Beijing cannot tolerate regionalism, as the process would complicate its goal of becoming the primary provider of security and development across Eurasia.

The fact remains that China's map of the world has no space for a distinct South Asia, nor does its policy accommodate a powerful regional actor like India. This is a pattern that has repeated itself around the world. American displacement in East Asia was only the beginning. In Eastern Europe, Beijing has effectively sidelined the EU through its 16+1 Forum, a grouping that includes the Eastern European states and China. Czech President Miloš Zeman has gone so far as to call his country an 'unsinkable aircraft carrier for China in Europe.'[14] And despite China's bonhomie with Russia in Central Asia, their economic relationship is fundamentally skewed to benefit China, while its gradually expanding military presence in the region is bound to cause a headache for Moscow.

THE PERFECT ALTERNATIVE

The question to ask, given these circumstances, is whether China's presence in South Asia is sustainable. Due to the absence of alternatives, the answer is almost certainly yes. For one thing, South Asia presents all the right ingredients for the Chinese economic model; densely populated emerging economies that are at a developmental stage, comparable to China a decade earlier. Beijing's unparalleled ability to boost industrial productivity, plug critical infrastructure gaps, create stable regulatory environments, and capitalize on the benefits of globalization would undoubtedly serve these states well. Additionally, as China moves up the value chain, several low-end manufacturing supply chains will relocate to countries with lower labour costs. Asia's frontier emerging markets like Bangladesh and Vietnam are best placed to take advantage of this trend. Also, given China's 'all of the government' approach, coordination and implementation delays are quite negligible. Unlike other countries, which rely on private business and extensive negotiation processes, Chinese money is often quick and easy. As early as 2008, the then-President of Senegal, Abdoulaye Wade, in a scathing criticism of Western institutions and lenders and in praise of China's development initiatives wrote, 'China has helped African nations build infrastructure projects in record time... a contract that would take five years to discuss, negotiate and sign with the World Bank takes three months when we have dealt with the Chinese authorities.'[15] This is a sentiment that is shared by many leaders of the developing world.

Secondly, the BRI presents South Asian countries an alternative to both India's preferences and the demands of the Western-led international order. Echoing China's long-standing desire to establish a 'new model of international relations' at the 2018 Central Conference on Work Relating to Foreign Affairs, Xi called on China to 'lead the reform of the global governance system with the concepts of fairness and justice.'[16] Developing countries, he said, are Beijing's 'natural allies' in this endeavour. Indeed, Beijing has spent significant diplomatic and monetary capital to incubate alternative governance propositions, as seen with the AIIB. Beijing's diplomatic rhetoric today has more to do with securing its own interests than necessarily improving the agency of developing states in international affairs. Yet, smaller countries, such as those in South Asia, are likely to embrace the possibilities of new global governance frameworks and institutions, if only because it improves bargaining power with existing ones. More importantly, Asian states deplore the political and governance conditions set by Western institutions and prefer China's 'no strings attached' approach. That China is willing to invest in countries with weak intellectual property (IP) laws, convoluted land rights, and several other political, legal and economic risks only gives it an added advantage over other investors.

Third, China's model for governance strengthens the state. For developing nations that have stronger state-led economies, China's experience with leveraging state-owned enterprises for development and growth is very relevant. The BRI only strengthens this emerging shift to state-led capitalism. Further, in those states with weak democratic norms and institutions, China's surveillance technologies are increasingly providing an attractive option for maintaining and consolidating political power. Research suggests that China is exporting such technologies in varying degrees to fifty-four countries across the political spectrum.[17] China's offering of robust state control combined with micro-political and economic freedoms has proven quite successful at transitioning a nation from low-end manufacturing to an innovation and knowledge-based economy—a leap that every state in South Asia is keen to make. The fact that China seeks to facilitate this process by investing in their development on a government-to-government basis, as opposed to a market-based approach, only enhances its appeal by reducing investment uncertainty and political influence through businesses or civil society.

The dynamics in South Asia ultimately boil down to a situation in which small states are in dire need of infrastructure, finance, and development, and China is currently the only appealing benefactor. Moreover, unlike for the East Asian nations, China's presence does not seem to pose a real security risk to smaller states in South Asia, so it is easier for them to buy the narrative that China's trade and investment will spur development and stability.

PUTTING THE NEIGHBOURHOOD FIRST AGAIN

It is clear that the nature of dynamics within the South Asian subcontinent has changed. For over seven decades, India was at the core of the region's political and economic networks. Over the past decade or so, that centre of gravity has shifted, with China now steering the ship. In many ways, this signals the death of a particular type of construct for South Asia, one that was defined by India's democratic credentials and potential for economic growth. As India fails to strengthen its position, the very identity of the subcontinent is being subsumed by the BRI. The question for India now is whether it can renegotiate the terms of its engagement with its neighbours in the face of rapidly changing geopolitical realities.

Perhaps India should take a leaf out of Deng Xiaoping's playbook and bide its time. It is worth noting that India's warning ahead of the BRI summit in May 2017, that Beijing's connectivity ambitions would exacerbate risk in the absence of good governance, has proven prophetic. A 2018 report concluded that for eight countries that have signed on to the BRI, including the Maldives and Sri Lanka, the projects are financially unsustainable and that strategic assets are being collateralized for debt repayment.[18] Beijing tends to supply massive credit through burdensome loans that ignore the well-established principles of financial sustainability and transparency. It seeks to open markets in developing countries to offload its industrial capacity without offering them the benefits of fair trade. Given that China favours working with regimes that suffer from democratic deficits, most recipient countries either lack the political will or the administrative capacity to analyse the long-term implications of China's investments, usually leaving future governments to deal with the consequences. As we have seen, this is a model that naturally lends itself to instability.

This dynamic has already played out in Southeast Asia. As he campaigned ahead of the 2018 Malaysian general election, Mahathir Mohamad deftly tapped into the resentment of Chinese investments in his country to build support. After his victory, Mahathir called the railway projects 'very damaging to the economy,' and said that Malaysia reserved the right to renegotiate terms on some of the contracts.[19] Domestic politics in South Asia reflect the consequences of this state of affairs. Mahinda Rajapaksa, who orchestrated the island state's China pivot, has supported protests that erupted over

Beijing's ownership of Hambantota Port.[20] Bangladesh blacklisted a key Chinese firm over financial irregularities and corruption charges.[21] Myanmar is reviewing China's $9-billion port project over financial concerns.[22] Even Pakistan, which considers Beijing an 'all-weather friend', is considering an IMF bailout because of external debt to China.[23] Increasingly, South Asian states themselves are coming to realize that Beijing's investments are not entirely benign.

For now, South Asian states are partnering with Beijing because it offers unparalleled commercial opportunities. What happens when the economic and political implications of the BRI become apparent to them? If anything, China's presence may well help India overcome its adversarial 'big brother' image in the region. Beijing's influence has also provided the impetus for India to reinvigorate its own initiatives. Media reports indicated that Delhi will adopt a three-pronged approach of 'tracking Beijing's activities; pursuing its own projects and commitments; and advising neighbours on the consequences of engaging with China.'[24] New Delhi has already indicated its intention to anchor 'a rules-based order' in the Indo-Pacific at the Shangri-La Dialogue in 2018. In a veiled criticism of China's practices, Prime Minister Modi warned that connectivity initiatives must 'empower nations, not place them under impossible debt burden'.[25]

In the long term, India's emphasis on recipient-led development frameworks, financial transparency, and benefits for local populations is likely to be a far more politically sustainable model. Thus, New Delhi will benefit if it merely waits. The fact that India will have emerged as the world's second-largest economy by the mid-century and that it is geographically central to the subcontinent will eventually make India a more potent partner than China. This is, however, dependent on New Delhi's willingness to shed its diffidence on regional trade and integration. India's lack of commitment to connectivity initiatives like BIMSTEC or trade agreements like the RCEP will damage its long-term ability to shape economic outcomes in the region. As India moves from a two- to ten-trillion-dollar economy in the coming decade, it must invest in its institutional capacity to deliver propositions and results. In time, India's organic capabilities will more effectively challenge China's presence.

It is also worth remembering that China is a 'lonely power' and its influence is limited to the domestic support it might find in smaller states. India, on the other hand, can bank on the Quadrilateral (Quad) Initiative to balance China's rise in the Indo-Pacific. The Quad Initiative itself was reborn soon after India's very vocal opposition to the BRI in May 2017. Before India's objection, the Trump administration had sent a senior member of the National Security Council to the Belt and Road Forum. A course correction soon followed after India's defiance. Shortly after visiting New Delhi, US defence secretary, James Mattis, testified at a congressional commission that 'in a globalized world, there ought to be many belts and many roads.'[26] Soon after, then US Secretary of State Rex Tillerson criticized what he called China's 'predatory economics' in Asia, and revealed that the US had initiated a 'quiet conversation', with its partners about challenging the BRI.[27] By November 2017, India, Australia, Japan and the US had aligned themselves with certain norms, development practices and security rules under the aegis of the Quad.

To be fair, the Quad itself is still muddling along and differences in geographical scope, military capacity, and political will continue to hinder cooperation. Indeed, observers were right to point out that it was slow to respond to the events in Male. However, the Quad remains a long-term vehicle. It has already met three times since 2017, even as trilateral and bilateral platforms and exercises continue to proliferate. India and Japan, for example, are partnering very closely in South Asia under the aegis of the Asia-Africa Growth Corridor. The US, meanwhile, is facilitating the flow of its considerable private industry capital into development projects in the region. Moreover, new alignments, such as the recently signed India-Indonesia Joint Vision for the Indo-Pacific,[28] indicate that the

Quad's normative and economic vision for the region is already taking root. It is fair to argue that in the long term the collective political will, economic statecraft, and diplomatic engagement of the Quad will have an edge over Beijing's unilateralism. India must position itself as the pivot of a free and open Indo-Pacific, making itself central to the web of relationships emerging in this region.

China would do well to learn lessons from its own experience in East Asia. Even though most ASEAN states were in security and commercial relationships with the US, the sheer size of Beijing's regional presence and the compulsions of geography have forced them to abandon American preferences. This is arguably the same dynamic that will play out in South Asia for India and China. If China retains the upper hand now, it is because the Middle Kingdom's economy dwarfs India's by a factor of five—a gap that India will rapidly close by 2050. The only way for India to maintain its influence in South Asia is to accept competition with China, instead of romanticizing a non-existent sphere of influence. India has done well to articulate the political and economic risks of China's investments. It must now walk the talk by invigorating its connectivity programmes, institutionalizing norms through regional forums like the Bay of Bengal Initiative for Multi-Sectoral Technical Economic Cooperation (BIMSTEC) and the Indian Ocean Rim Association (IORA), and increasing cooperation with the Quad. If India cannot provide an alternative roadmap for regional integration and development in South Asia, its ambition of being a leading power in the international system will stand on fragile footing.

New Delhi will also have to reimagine its relationship with China. It must recognize the long-term political threat from China, prepare to respond to Beijing's assertiveness in the medium term, and embrace China economically in the short term. In this, New Delhi would do well to draw from China's own experiences with the US. For decades, China benefited from financial flows and economic interdependence with the US. It never lost sight of the fact that the US would remain a long-term geopolitical rival. Today, the US finds itself competing with a power whose economy it was principally responsible for strengthening. India must replicate this model with China by creating economic interdependencies, while responding to political muscularity.

Keep in mind that these prescriptions are long-term. The fact remains that South Asia's developing economies are unlikely to reject investments under the BRI, even though they may come to resent some of the financial implications. Despite attempts to streamline their economic policies, neither India nor the Quad currently possesses the political will or the policy levers to invest with China's scale and velocity. Convergence on finance mechanisms and vehicles is also limited in the Quad. India, for example, is not part of a US-Australia-Japan infrastructure fund for the Indo-Pacific. Still, it would be amiss for observers of South Asian politics to view the region as a zero-sum game between China and India. Instead, the region is likely to witness several realignments in the coming decades, and domestic politics will influence these decisions as much as Indian or Chinese actions. Indeed, the events in the Maldives go to show that while China can hardwire its influence faster than any other country, the velocity of its involvement often precipitates economic and social risk, as well as domestic pushback. In the immediate future, however, developing countries will remain invested in their commercial partnerships with China.

VII

BEYOND THE BELT AND ROAD–PATHWAYS TO GLOBAL POWER

The Belt and Road Initiative is not just a connectivity project: it is also an announcement of China's resolve to be a global power. To do this, China employs a plethora of tools. A complete understanding of the BRI, then, also requires an understanding of China's evolving international engagement. There are three discernible foreign-policy tools that China employs, sometimes through the BRI and other times alongside it: first, China intends to influence international institutions; second, China is expanding its discourse power; and finally, Beijing is building a network of military partnerships.

A more detailed examination of these efforts gives us a glimpse into what global leadership with Chinese characteristics will look like in the future. Before that, however, consider just one example: the arrest of Meng Hongwei, the President of Interpol.[1] This was done under dubious circumstances in Beijing. Meng was the head of an international organization, and, ostensibly, independent of China's control. Nevertheless, Chinese authorities did not think twice about the global implications of his arrest. While we will explore the consequences of this event in more detail, China's message to the world was clear: even as China would participate in, and actively shape international order, it would be on the terms set by the Communist Party. This was a remarkable evolution in China's foreign policy. Under Mao, China was mostly an antagonist to the international order, and refused to acknowledge the legitimacy of its structures or norms. Under Deng, Hu and Jiang, China gradually conformed, in limited forms and measures. With Xi at the helm, however, China is employing a more extensive array of tools to influence and shape the international order. The motivations for using these tools are straightforward. As State Councillor Yang Jiechi explains, it had become 'increasingly difficult for Western governance concepts, systems, and models to keep up with the new international situation'.[2] Jiechi was perhaps giving voice to what was increasingly a common refrain in China's elite circles: the West was now in decline, and China could step up. According to Shiping Tang, data from China's academic journals database reveals that before the 2008 financial crisis, the phrases 'international order' or 'world order' appeared in articles about 14.3 times per year.[3] Since then, however, that number has nearly doubled to 27.8 times per year—indicating a growing awareness of China's position of strength in the international order.

The relationship between these academic discussions and government policy is difficult to ascertain. However, as Xi's early speeches on global governance show, the shift in tone and tenor of China's foreign-policy thinking was no coincidence. At the Central Conference on Work Relating to Foreign Affairs in 2014, Xi prioritized creating a 'more enabling international environment' for China's growth by 'developing a distinctive diplomatic approach befitting its role as a major country'.[4] In other words, Xi wanted to 'conduct diplomacy with salient Chinese features and a Chinese vision'. He elaborated on these themes again at two Politburo study sessions on global governance in 2015, where the common refrain was that the international balance of power was changing rapidly. Xi declared that China must occupy the 'commanding heights' of international affairs and 'must make the international order more reasonable and just, to protect the common interests of China and other developing countries'.[5]

Elaborating on some of Xi's pronouncements, Kevin Rudd argues that China's conceptualization of the world can be distilled into three interrelated concepts: the 'international order', which refers to institutions like the UN and the World Bank, the 'international system', which is the (primarily American) network of alliances and partnerships that underpin this order, and 'global governance', which signifies the working of this setup.[6] According to Rudd, China accepts the order itself, but rejects both the network of Western-led partnerships and how they function. Xi is determined to reform these systems by amplifying China's agency. According to him, the world wants to 'hear China's voice' and 'engage with China's solutions'.[7] This has led to three key foreign-policy actions taken by China: more emphasis on co-opting international organizations; expanding China's discourse power; and creating a new web of security partnerships that will entrench a Chinese-led international order.

CO-OPTING INTERNATIONAL ORGANIZATIONS

The expansion of China's influence in existing international institutions, the ascent of Chinese nationals within them, and the desire to create new ones as needed, have been driven as much by practical needs as by China's desire for symbolic recognition. Indeed, as a by-product of its rise, some institutions have welcomed China. The United Nations International Civil Aviation Organization (ICAO), for example, is currently managed by Liu Fang—a Chinese national.[8] As a country primed to host the world's largest aviation market by 2025,[9] it benefits the industry to have leadership with experience in China. Similarly, the World Bank appointed a Chinese national, Shaolin Yang, as its second-in-command; this was after resolving Beijing's long-standing resentment against the decision-making structure of global financial organizations.[10]

In fact, for a country that is considered a revisionist power, official policy statements and speeches from Chinese documents and leaders point to the importance Beijing attaches to global institutions—even those incubated and managed by the West. Still, if the Meng incident makes anything clear, it is that China's global efforts to occupy leadership positions in international organizations is far from benign. And while China can appear deeply involved in some organizations, it may resist others, and may even reject processes in existing ones.

Between these extreme behaviours, China seeks to project its own ideas and norms through its discursive agenda in international institutions. Consider, for example, the case of China in the UN. In 2017, two UN draft resolutions on the prevention of an arms race in outer space adopted the idea of shaping 'a community of shared future for mankind'. While most foreign press missed the significance of this news, Chinese officials believed that this 'showcase[d] China's responsibility as a major country'.[11] Examples like this are now multiplying, allowing China to implicate the normative underpinnings of the United Nations. For instance, in March 2018, China introduced a resolution seeking 'mutually beneficial cooperation in the field of human rights'. This was a first-of-its-kind statement emerging from China.[12] According to the Human Rights Watch, however, 'there is not even one mention of the word "individual" in the resolution, nor do the terms "human rights defender" or "civil society" appear'.[13] Instead, the resolution showcased Beijing's interest in reframing the relationship between individuals and the state, and gave primacy to the latter in human rights. The resolution also invoked Xi's ideas on the 'community of shared destiny', which entrenched Chinese conceptions into standard UN lingua franca. The concept, which was first introduced in the eighteenth National Congress work report, has gradually become an official catchphrase for China's leadership role in global governance.

More worryingly, China's design is taking shape even as democracies in other parts of the world appear unwilling or unable to support international institutions that they had incubated. Not only has the Trump administration announced its withdrawal from the UN Human Rights Council, UNESCO, and other institutions, but it is also cutting funding for the UN as a whole. China, meanwhile, is only beginning to expand its reach into the organization. Its preferred means include spending large sums of money and actively participating in the institution's agenda process. For example, China alone contributed nearly a tenth of the UN's peacekeeping budget, with another $1 billion in the pipeline for the next half a decade.[14] China has also provided nearly 8,000 PLA troops for peacekeeping missions.[15] This is part of a concerted strategy in China to work through existing institutions, often to subvert norms and processes and to attain leadership status.

Occupying leadership positions in international organizations also paves the way for the enforcement of Beijing's domestic agenda. The arbitrary arrest of Hongwei was hardly the only reason Beijing's leadership of Interpol has been controversial. Under Hongwei's charge, China had effectively abused Interpol's red notice system to target dissidents, activists and generally anyone who upset the Communist Party. The Human Rights Watch has documented multiple instances of such abuse, including the practice of threatening family members of dissidents who reside abroad.[16] More often than not, China successfully employed Interpol's system to act against individuals it deemed were adversely affecting its 'core national interests', whether on the subject of Taiwanese independence or sensitive issues such as Tibet and Xinjiang. Similarly, in January 2017, Xi and Margaret Chan, then director-general of the World Health Organization (WHO), agreed to bring a global health focus to economic development, with the BRI receiving the bulk of the attention.[17] Not only does this give China a more significant role in shaping global development outcomes, but it also legitimizes the BRI across multiple international organizations whose members may not have signed on to China's propositions under the initiative.

Later, in 2017, China had aggressively positioned Qian Tang as the head of the United Nations Educational, Scientific and Cultural Organization (UNESCO)—an organization Chinese officials see as a vehicle to regulate the Internet. In 2013, for example, countries like China, Cuba, Venezuela and Russia passed a resolution that asked the UNESCO to engage 'strategically in the international debates concerning cyberspace in the coming years'. In an interview with *Foreign Policy*, Tang even admitted that he hoped 'UNESCO could provide a stage for the world to wrestle with ways to strike the proper balance between free expression, privacy, and the need to prevent abuses of the Internet by extremists'.[18] While Tang ultimately withdrew his candidacy, it didn't change the fact that Chinese nationals were already heading key institutions that managed the Internet. Houlin Zhao , for example, is the secretary-general of the International Telecommunication Union (ITU) and has repeatedly expressed the need for Chinese companies to actively participate in the making of international telecommunication standards that enable them to take initiatives in future market competition.[19]

China is also playing a more active role in setting the agenda in international institutions. Since hosting the 2014 Asia Pacific Economic Conference (APEC), Chinese scholars and policymakers have increasingly highlighted their country's efforts in shaping global agendas and rule-setting priorities. China hosting the G20 summit in 2016 is another significant milestone cited by Chinese officials. Foreign minister Wang Yi, for example, highlighted the fact that the G20 formulated guiding principles and mechanisms to cope with issues such as economic growth, multilateral investment and climate change, with guidance from Xi.[20] He has also praised Chinese efforts to set rules and agendas in international organizations to deal with emerging challenges such as space, cyberspace and the polar regions.[21] *The People's Daily* insisted that China's involvement in the G20 coincided with the 'decreasing efficiency' in 'international economic mechanisms with the Group of Seven (G7) as the centre'.[22]

Finally, China seeks to build alternative institutions like the AIIB, which represents China's capacity and inclination to create a new, parallel institutional order. However, as Beijing's behaviour in Western institutions suggests, China is not so much constructing a parallel order as it is diversifying its stake in the existing one. While there is little question that the AIIB provides China with a new tool to enhance its multilateral influence, the fact remains that the Middle Kingdom has, so far at least, allowed the AIIB to cooperate with existing institutions. This is not to say that the AIIB is not significant—it represents China's capability in creating alternatives when existing mechanisms do not align with its own interests. More importantly, the AIIB allows China to crowd-finance from other institutions. And when Chinese investments go sour in host countries, China relies on these funders—which includes Western multilateral banks and organizations like the IMF—to bail our debt-ridden countries.

China's behaviour in international organizations is quite pragmatic. For years, Chinese leaders have consistently maintained that today's international order has not been sufficiently diverse in design or decision-making. However, the desire for order itself is equally prominent. The international liberal order is antithetical to China's ambition. Indeed, Beijing is well aware of how Washington has employed international institutions as a force to multiply its own power. The question, therefore, is whether China will adjust its behaviour to respect international norms and rules. Meng's detention reveals that the opposite is likely to be true. China will alter the behaviour of other states and international institutions in the international order, and China's international role will always be subordinate to the diktat of the Communist Party.

MEDIA, DIASPORA AND SOFT POWER

Under Xi, China has also strengthened its ability to seize discursive power. It has elevated the objective of propagating China's voice to the global level. In all fairness, this is not one of China's new ambitions. As early as 2004, Hu Jintao had stressed the need for China to enhance its cultural soft power, and enshrined this idea as an official tool of statecraft in his 2007 report to Congress.[23] Similarly, Xi made enhancing cultural power an early priority in his presidency. At the third plenary session of the eighteenth Central Committee, a resolution titled 'Heighten Cultural Openness' directed the Party to build communication skills through a 'system of discourse with the outside world'.[24] According to Chinese scholars, 'discourse power' refers to 'the influence generated by the logic, values, and ideologies contained in a nation's discussions and public discourse',[25] while simultaneously carrying connotations of the right of states to 'speak' in international affairs. In other words, China not only wanted greater space for its own 'voice', it also wanted to condition other states' understanding of China's communication idiosyncrasies. It is worth pointing out that under Hu, cultural power was not merely a matter of international relations. In his work report to the 2007 Congress, Hu stressed that this was also a domestic goal. 'Enhancing cultural soft power,' the report noted, 'is a basic requirement for realizing scientific development and social harmony. It is necessary for satisfying rising demands for spiritual culture and national development strategy.'[26] Xi, however, has more explicitly linked soft power to achieving China's foreign policy goals.[27]

As part of this effort, he has revitalized the United Front Work Department (UFWD)—an organization whose foundation can be traced back to Mao Zedong. Once called the 'magic weapon' by Mao, the UFWD is a secretive and anonymous organization that projects Beijing's voice and soft power push. Its explicit aim is to shape a favourable environment for the Communist Party's political agenda and to influence opinion on China abroad. Under Xi, the CCP held its first Central Committee Conference on United Front Work in decades, and established a leading group on UFWD with Xi at the helm, providing 'a direct line of command from the [CCP] Politburo to [the] United Front'.[28] Since then, more than 40,000 individuals have been added to the cadre. In his address to the nineteenth National Congress, Xi called United Front work 'an important way to ensure the success of the [Chinese Communist] Party's cause'.[29] Echoing Mao, Xi suggested that the the United Front work was a 'magic weapon' that was important for bringing about 'the great rejuvenation of the Chinese nation'—explicitly tying this organization's objectives with those of China's global ambitions.[30]

INSTRUMENTS OF DISCOURSE

Under Xi, the Communist Party and the United Front have used the state media to sway Western educational institutions and influence local political parties to shape the international environment. State-controlled media is Xi's primary tool for shaping international discourse. Back in 2014, he hinted at the creation of a new type of mainstream media that would be powerful, influential, and credible. This pronouncement was actuated at the National People's Congress on March 2018, which saw the consolidation of government media work under the Central Propaganda Department. Organizationally, China Central Television, China Radio International, and China National Radio were merged into the 'Voice of China'.[31] Well before this build-up of China's state media's overseas reach, Xi reminded the world that the press run by the party and the government were propaganda fronts and must have the party as their 'family name'.[32]

As part of a more global effort, earlier in 2017, the official state broadcaster, CCTV, was rebranded into the China Global Television Network (CGTN)—an organization Xi entrusted with the responsibility of telling China's story well. Chinese observers describe a strategy known as 'borrow a boat to go out on the ocean', employed for this purpose, where Chinese media outlets enter strategic partnerships with foreign media to pay for CCP authorized content.[33] Several prominent European newspapers, such as Germany's *Handelsblatt* and the UK's *Telegraph* and *Daily Mail*, now carry paid media inserts. In the US, reports indicate that the Party now provides paid advertisements in major newspapers like the *Boston Globe*, *The Wall Street Journal* and *The Washington Post*. These efforts only represent China's intent to amplify its voice in major democracies. A *Financial Times* investigation suggests that at least two hundred Chinese language publications were now broadcasting content to millions of readers globally.[34]

Simultaneously, Beijing also pressures foreign media and academic organizations to censor sensitive conversations in exchange for market access. Freedom House reports that since Xi came to power, China has negatively affected freedom of expression outside China over forty times in seventeen countries and institutions.[35] In October 2017, for example, the German publication agency Springer, known for its publications such as *Nature* and *Scientific American*, withdrew over a thousand articles that related to topics sensitive to the CCP such as Taiwan, Tibet and human rights.[36] Earlier in 2017, even Cambridge University Press nearly acquiesced to Beijing's demands, agreeing to pull down 'over 300 sensitive articles and book reviews from its website in China' under threat of having to shut down their operations in China. Only after pressure from academic groups in the transatlantic community did Cambridge reverse its decision.[37]

Apart from attempting to influence the global media landscape, China is spending over $10 billion a year to promote academic exchanges and cultural programmes.[38] The most concrete manifestation of this programme is China's Confucius Institutes, which are research institutions hosted in foreign universities. Reports indicate that there are now nearly 600 such institutes around the world. Increasingly, however, evidence emerging from Western democracies suggests that these institutions are significantly straining academic freedom in universities, and are emerging as crucial to Beijing's overseas surveillance efforts. In 2017, the US National Association of Scholars released a detailed report on Confucius institutes, saying that these organizations require host universities to avoid 'tarnish[ing] the reputation of the Confucius Institutes'; regularly intimidate faculty, who now 'face pressure to self-censor'; and 'monitor, intimidate, and harass Chinese students'.[39]

This is not surprising. The Politburo's top propaganda official, Li Changchun, once boasted in 2009 that the Confucius Institutes were an essential part of China's overseas propaganda setup.[40] These organizations now enable China to monitor both the attitudes of foreign countries as well as its diaspora. Once again, this is part of Chairman Xi's efforts to project China's influence abroad, and strengthen the Party's grip over everything related to China. At a national work meeting held on February 2017, for example, he called for 'closely uniting' with overseas Chinese in support of the Chinese dream[41]—a phrase that was later incorporated into the nineteenth report of the Party Work Congress. In fact, China has now established an Overseas Chinese Affairs Office in Beijing, which is responsible for guiding ethnic Chinese organizations abroad by 'infiltrating their inner workings without overtly intervening; and to influence through guidance, rather than openly leading them'.[42]

China also now invests in overseas cells of the Communist Party, which are responsible for promoting Party and government policies. Beijing employs these cells to prioritize political party ties with countries. Western soft power approaches generally rely on civil society interactions. These efforts have allowed Beijing to expand its convening power, and increase the legitimacy of the CPC in the domestic conversations of other countries. At the first edition of the 'CPC in Dialogue with World Political Parties', Xi called on the CCP to 'work with other political parties around the world' to advance China's goal of 'building of a community of common destiny'.[43] Xi added that in the coming five years, the CCP intends to invite 15,000 members of foreign political parties to China for exchanges. China's interactions with the political elite of a country significantly enable the socialization and legitimization of its foreign policy. For example, former British Prime Minister David Cameron now leads a joint British-Chinese initiative known as the UK-China Fund, which promotes the BRI in Europe.[44] Similarly, Australian Labour politician Bob Carr now leads the Australia-China Relations Institute—an organization that promotes the BRI, and is linked to donations from the United Front.[45] Research and documentation reveal that this is a story that has repeated itself in Eastern Europe, Central Asia, Latin America and in South and Southeast Asia.[46]

SHARP POWER—TO PIERCE, PENETRATE AND PERFORATE

In pursuing soft power with Chinese characteristics, Beijing has forced democracies to reconceptualize their understanding of how power functions. China's actions go well beyond promoting a benign cultural presence; and constitute instead 'sharp' power, in 'the sense that they pierce, penetrate, or perforate the political and information environments in the targeted countries'.[47] The phrase was initially coined by the US National Endowment for Democracy (NED), which insists that China's end goal is not to 'win hearts and minds' as much as it is to manipulate the information ecosystem around the audience it seeks to influence. While the report is worth reading for the extensive documentation of China's sharp power in countries ranging from Argentina to Poland, the most visibly aggressive and blatant examples of China's operations come from Australia.

Australia deserves special attention because of its relationship with both China and the US. For the past decade, Australia has delicately balanced its close economic interdependence with China and its historical security ties with the US. Under Xi, this balance was becoming increasingly untenable as the security situation in the SCS—along with broader disagreements about the international order between China and the US—burst into the open. Following this, in 2015, the Australian Security Intelligence Organization (ASIO) warned both the Labour and Conservative parties in Australia that some of their largest donors had 'strong connections to the Chinese Communist Party' and that their 'donations might come with strings attached'.[48] Media reports suggest that the depth of Chinese influence was so much that political figures from both parties continued to accept hundreds of thousands of dollars from suspicious donors. The Melbourne Law School estimates that for the past fifteen years, nearly 80 per cent of all foreign political donations to Australia have been from Chinese sources.[49]

The most notorious case was that of Labour Party Senator Sam Dastyari, with Australian investigations revealing that he had regurgitated China's official line on the SCS in exchange for donations from a Chinese national with strong ties to the Party.[50] Chinese influence operations in Australia deserve attention, if only because they remain so overt. They signal the high level of risk the CCP is willing to expose itself to in order to influence democratic processes and norms. In fact, even though Australia has now passed some of the most sweeping foreign interference legislation in any democracy, China's influence remains strong and overt.[51] Even as the central government doubled down on China's interference, the Australian state of Victoria signed a memorandum of understanding (MoU) with the CCP on the BRI, without explicit oversight from the central government. The Communist Party, it appears, had exploited political loopholes in Australia's federal relationship. *The China Daily* later praised the state government for this move, noting that 'while Canberra deals more with issues related to national security and ideology, local governments tend to be more practical in their cooperation'.[52] Moreover, while Australia is possessed of the institutional capacity and political will to respond to China's behaviour, other countries like New Zealand, which is another hotbed for Chinese influence operations, remain ill prepared and underequipped to identify and counter them.[53] China's projection of media power—either to advance its own voice, to curtail the views of others, or to intimidate and browbeat opposition—marks a significant change in how global powers project influence.

NEW MILITARY COALITIONS

While rising influence in international organizations along with China's (sharp) power constitute the softer edge of Beijing's global ambition, its military activities also deserve attention. The rapid expansion of Beijing's commercial and political interests around the world is compelling China to project force and influence outwards. Xi first articulated this imperative at the Central Work Conference on Foreign Affairs in 2014, calling for 'ardently protecting China's overseas interests' and strengthening China's capability to do so.[54] This ambition was first articulated in China's 2015 Defence White Paper and, more recently, in the 2019 iteration of this document. The 2019 White Paper now more explicitly links becoming a global security power to Xi's 'China Dream'.

Unsurprisingly, China's more outward-facing national-security policy was first articulated in the context of its rising power in Asia. At the 2014 summit of the Conference on Interaction and Confidence Building Measures in Asia (CICA)—a regional institution to which the US is not a party—Xi argued that Asian states should handle Asian security problems.[55] At the time, this was a response to America's rebalance in Asia. Since then, however, he has signalled a more global ambition: in a February 2017 meeting of China's new National Security Commission, he called on the country's national security elite to increase cooperation and guide the international community in building an international security order.[56] He explicitly called for a global vision of the national security policy and promised to build China's comprehensive national capabilities to achieve this goal.

China's rise as a military power first began with its rapid entry into the global arms markets. As of 2017, China was the fourth-largest arms supplier in the world: it exported $25 billion worth of defence equipment.[57] To some extent, China's behaviour in the arms market is purely economic. During the Iran-Iraq conflict, for example, China exported arms to both countries. However, China has long linked the supply of arms to its foreign policy objectives—a trend that has become more pronounced. From North Africa—where Western suppliers are absent—to states like Pakistan, Bangladesh and Myanmar in Asia, China's arms exports have followed and supported its political interests. This suggests that China is learning from America's playbook and understands that defence trade often leads to more political influence.

Arms exports aside, the most visible indication of China's global rise is the formalization of its first overseas military presence in Djibouti; China claims that this presence will aid its UN peacekeeping responsibilities and anti-piracy operations in the Gulf of Aden. However, official policy documents, along with high-level statements, make it clear that China's overseas presence has an active link to both its economic statecraft through the BRI, as well as its ability to shape its external security environment. According to the Chinese Academy of Military Sciences, for example, the BRI 'provides not only the overseas space for China's national interests' expansion but also a practice model for maintaining overseas interest.[58] Elaborating on this strategy, Chinese foreign-policy experts suggest that Xi's foreign policy has been characterized as a synthesis of military and economic strategy to achieve the two centenary goals.

Xi first articulated many of these themes at the Work Conference on Neighbourhood Policy. Here he argued for 'synchronized progress' in economic and security cooperation to support China's vision for Asian security.[59] This idea has become the defining template for China's acquisition of overseas military facilities. Indeed, Djibouti was likely only the first amongst many in China's network of ports and other critical infrastructure likely to be used for military purposes. Already, for example, China has stirred controversy in the Pacific, having approached the island state of Vanuatu to build a permanent military presence in the region.[60] While ministers from the state, along with China's embassy, have stated that the news is baseless, observers from regional democracies like Japan and Australia are visibly shaken. Similar ambitions surround Pakistan's deep seaport of Gwadar, which has already seen visits from Chinese submarines. In fact, the *South China Morning Post* reported that senior security officials from Beijing were seized of the need 'to set up another base in Gwadar for its warships because Gwadar is now a civilian port'.[61]

While overseas military bases undoubtedly are the most tangible outcomes of China's emerging security policy, Beijing has also expended significant political capital on building security relationships. This follows from the 2015 Military Foreign Affairs Work Conference, where Xi heralded a new phase of military diplomacy.[62] The 2015 and 2019 Defence White Paper later called on the PLA to 'actively expand military and security cooperation' and 'to build a regional security cooperation architecture'.[63] These shifts, once again, stem from the 2014 foreign-policy work conference, where Chairman Xi prioritized building a 'global network of partnerships'. Evidence strongly suggests that Beijing is supporting policy statements through intense administrative action. According to scholars, almost half of all bilateral exchanges between Beijing and other countries are led by military officials, with Asia accounting for over 40 per cent of all military to military exchanges. China's actions in this regard have gradually gained momentum in other parts of the world as well—even though China proceeds at a different pace with different actors. In 2018, for example, China hosted its first China-Africa Defence and Security Forum, a two-week event that brought together some of the highest-ranking officials from forty-nine African nations for a dialogue with Beijing.[64] China has also emulated Western military institutions in its zeal to welcome serving officers from friendly nations. According to Elizabeth Economy, the PLA runs over sixty military academies that train over a thousand foreign officers every year.[65] Latin American countries, she notes, have been the primary beneficiaries of this administrative arrangement. In Southeast Asia, China is also pushing for members of ASEAN to hold joint military drills in the SCS—a development that follows America's decision to remove China from the annual Rim of the Pacific (RIMPAC) exercises.[66] China also conducts more military-to-military exercises now than ever before; according to the US Department of Defence, in 2017, it conducted at least twenty such bilateral and multilateral activities.[67]

Finally, Beijing now also hosts key international forums and invests in regional organizations that can amplify its own security concepts. Xi, for example, used the CICA to unveil his 'Asia for Asians' security concept—a move widely believed to have been a response to the Obama administration's 'Pivot to Asia'. China later prolonged its leadership of the institution from 2014 to 2018. The forum itself provided China with the ability to challenge American influence over security conversations in East and Southeast Asia. China has similarly utilized the Shanghai Cooperation Organization (SCO) to promote its security interests in the Eurasian landmass. It often advances agendas of terrorism and cybersecurity that would fail to pass muster in the UN. Beijing actively shapes the agenda of SCO members in other security conversations as well, with research suggesting that SCO members are increasingly voting as a block at the UN. More importantly, the grouping is advancing a model for security cooperation that overlaps with NATO. Both Armenia and Azerbaijan, for example, are now dialogue partners for the SCO, despite enjoying close political and military ties with NATO. Turkey's President Erdogan appears to be going down the same route, publicly calling for Ankara to forget NATO and seek closer ties with the SCO for Eurasian integration instead. Similarly, China now hosts the Xiangshan Forum, a security dialogue set up to rival the Shangri-La Dialogue, which Beijing sees as a forum Washington and its allies use to gang up on China.[68] Defence officials, military leaders and international organizations gathered at this Forum in 2018 to discuss 'building a new type of security and partnership featuring equality, mutual trust, and win-win cooperation'— this is China's lingo for describing the norms of a Chinese security order.

A NEW ALIGNMENT BETWEEN RUSSIA AND CHINA

Perhaps no other partnership has been as convenient for China as its alliance with Russia. In September 2018, both countries sent a powerful signal about their strengthening partnership with China's participation in Russia's military exercise in Vostok.[69] While China's 3,000-strong delegation paled in comparison to the 300,000 troops that Moscow included in the exercises, Vostok was a powerful sign of a new alignment between Russia and China. Significantly, both countries have increasingly sought to involve each other in their own security hotspots. In 2016, for example, navies from Moscow and Beijing participated in joint drills in the SCS;[70] in 2017, both nations participated in exercises in the Baltic Sea.[71] Both countries have also signalled their intention to intensify military cooperation in the Arctic—an emerging strategic geography. Most recently, both China and Russia conducted a first-of-its-kind joint air patrol in East Asia. It was provocative enough for South Korea to fire 'hundreds of warning shots'.[72] A strong convergence on global issues has supported these military ties. In September 2018, for example, Xi and Russian President Vladimir Putin promised to 'align their positions on major international and regional issues.'[73] Both countries have increasingly supported each other's position on international security at the UN, with China aping Moscow's positions on Syria and receiving Russian support in the SCS. Both are also now actively involved in pushing for a 'cyber code of conduct' in international organizations in an attempt to vest governments with greater control over the Internet. Moscow and Beijing have also largely defied American sanctions against Iran, with Xi increasing the purchase of oil and Moscow supplying military weapons to Iran.

Beijing's gradual build-up of its military footprint, coupled with a new network of partnerships, will test the international security order underpinned by American primacy. China is now a formidable presence in the Indo-Pacific, in the Eurasian landmass, and in the Arctic. While the exact shape of China's global military ambitions remains uncertain, it is clear that powerful drivers are animating its strategy, whether they are commercial, domestic or related to the international order itself. In conjunction with the BRI, these capabilities will give China greater leverage to shape and transform the international order.

LIVING IN THE HOUSE THE US BUILT

For years, China has benefited from global public goods provided by the international order—whether it is free trade or international security. However, the consensus in China appears to be that the grip of Western powers on the international order is fraying; this opinion was only bolstered by the election of Trump and the polarization that followed Brexit. While the BRI is Beijing's most concerted, multifaceted and ambitious tool towards claiming a global leadership role, it is supported by China's efforts to reclaim discourse power in international institutions, amplify China's voice in international affairs, and re-imagine the global security framework.

When asked about Beijing's long-term goal, Chairman Xi answered that China wanted to actively take part in reforming and constructing the global governance system, and 'ensure that the world political and economic order develops in a more just and reasonable direction'.[74] Even as Beijing pursues this ambition, however, it is clear that it remains committed to the *infrastructure* of the current international order—that is, it continues to support the UN, the WTO and so on. It is the *software* that China would rather change. Increasingly, it is clear that the Middle Kingdom will continue to inject more Chinese elements into the international order. The result, for the mid-term at least, is an uneasy coexistence between the international order underwritten by a Western consensus, and an emerging alternative from China. Wang Yi insists that China's efforts to reform governance systems are not an attempt to overthrow the past, but to create reform and innovation and keep pace with the times. As the next chapter will show, these efforts are coinciding with, and driving, some of the most momentous transformations in the world order since the fall of the Berlin Wall.

VIII

THREE COLLISIONS AND THE END OF THE LIBERAL WORLD ORDER

The international liberal order is undoubtedly going through a period of tumult, epitomized by the stunning victory of Trump in November 2016. Through out his campaign, Trump repudiated some of the most long-standing and deeply entrenched principles of American domestic politics and foreign policy that have come to define the post-war order as we know it. He vocally blamed globalization for the ills plaguing US workers and repeatedly questioned the utility of America's system of military alliances in Europe and Asia. The US presidential campaign was also heavily polarized, in part due to the personalities involved, and in part due to the impact of social media and information communication technologies. Unsurprisingly, the morning after his victory, a *New York Times* editorial argued that Trump 'will plunge the US into an era of unknowns that has little parallel in the nation's 240-year history'.[1] The foreign policy establishment in Washington supported this dire assessment. In the popular magazine *Foreign Affairs*, thirty-two experts were asked this question: 'Is the liberal order is in peril?' Twenty-six respondents suggested it was.[2]

It is important to note, however, that American primacy was eroding well before the American people voted Trump into office. A few weeks before Trump assumed presidency, the American intelligence community released a report that forecasted a tectonic shift in international affairs: It predicted the end of American dominance and the decline of the post-war international order.[3] It is hard to pinpoint the exact reason for this decline. Some blame American policy itself—either for its excesses post 9/11, or the disastrous consequences of the 2008 financial crisis. Others point to a more global phenomenon: the gradual diffusion of wealth and power to the East. Whatever the cause, it is clear that a new order is upon us. For the first time since 1945, the chief architect of the international order is no longer proactively advocating for human rights, free markets, or common security measures.

Even if Trump is to win a second term in 2020, the consequences of these momentous shifts will far outlast his administration. 'The liberal international order,' as it is often known, is unlikely to bounce back to what it was in the late twentieth century. A new order is fast emerging, and its contours and implications are still unknown. It will certainly not resemble anything built in the twentieth century, as the world is more networked, connected and interdependent than ever before. This reality will coexist with the onset of multiple power centres, each with their own guiding impulses. At least three immediate trends are implicating a new order: First, the emergence of new strategic geographies that will require new systems of management. Second, the gradual erosion of the distinction between the virtual and the real domains. Finally, the disruptions facing the global economy and a new economic proposition that is gaining traction.

THE COLLISION OF THREE GEOGRAPHIES[4]

Perhaps the most macro-perspective on the changing world order is our recasting of our mental maps. Today's order is best characterized as an extension of the Atlantic System. Broadly put, the Atlantic Charter—a joint document signed by US President Franklin D. Roosevelt and UK Prime Minister Winston Churchill in August 1941—is often seen as the founding document of the liberal international order. In many ways, it provided the foundational norms and principles upon which the world would be organized—including people's right to self-determination, equal access to trade, freedom of navigation at sea, and the establishment of a permanent system for collective security.[5] The famous American political scientist Walter Lippmann best described this system in 1943: 'The Atlantic Ocean is not the frontier between Europe and the Americas. It is the inland sea of a community of nations allied with one another by geography, history, and vital necessity.'[6]

Today, the diffusion of power towards the East, new interdependencies of global economic and migratory flows, the adoption and diffusion of new technologies and the geopolitical interests of rising powers have left the Atlantic system incapable of managing the world order. The question, then, is where will the new world order be born? Westphalian norms, for example, were born as a unique product of European histories and geopolitics. Imperial China's tributary system was a product of hierarchical relationships in East Asia. Pax Britannica was the first 'global' order, built on strong commercial and strategic foundations—these are the same foundations that America inherited after the World War II. Today, these foundations are crumbling, and a new international order is being born amidst the collision of three hitherto distinct geographies.

The first collision, which is already well under way, is the union of the Indian and Pacific oceans. A new network of military partnerships and new flows of trade and energy routes have dramatically increased the interactions of states from East Asia to East Africa, creating what Japanese Prime Minister Shinzo Abe once called 'the confluence of two seas'.[7] Popularly defined as the Indo-Pacific, it is a construct encouraged by the rise of China but defined in equal measure by regional actors responding to Beijing's proposition. Maritime Asia is now larger than the US, ASEAN and China—these regions were earlier organized under the Asia-Pacific construct. However, now, this frontier is not limited to the eastern Indian Ocean. While China and the US will remain the most indispensable actors in the Indo-Pacific, powers like India, Japan and Australia are stitching together their own matrix of cooperation in the region. The interactions of these 'big' powers with emerging ones—such as Indonesia, South Africa and Iran—will similarly influence the course of this region.

The second is the conflation of Europe and Asia into one coherent strategic system—or what Zbigniew Brzezinski once called the chessboard of geopolitics: Eurasia.[8] This is an old idea, steeped in history. Today, this region has wider dimensions and a new vocabulary. The interaction of markets and communities from these once-separated geographies is creating a new super-continental-sized interdependence. Yet this interdependence is not without friction: China's shadow looms large over Europe, and its promise to underwrite the continent's prosperity has proved too difficult to resist. The EU itself is befuddled by migration from West Asia and uncertainty about its partnership with the US in this new geography. Moscow, meanwhile, is exhibiting a new zeal to reclaim its place as the archetypical Eurasian player even as members of NATO continue to bicker over their future role in the region. As these geopolitical tectonic plates both clash and merge, it is clear that East and West will set new terms of engagement. In other words, conceptualizing a new 'World-Island'—British geographer Halford Mackinder's phrase for Eurasia—is no longer mere speculation.

Finally, we have the Arctic: born as an unintended consequence of climate change, this geography will, for the first time, merge the politics of the Atlantic and the Pacific, even as it stimulates a clash between the arrangements that exist in these regions. Thanks to global warming, the Northern Sea Route is becoming a reality. The importance, as Russian President Putin declared as early as 2011, is that 'the shortest route between Europe's largest markets and the Asia-Pacific region lie[s] across the Arctic'.[9] The emergence of this geography, however, will be far from frictionless, and may well create a new distribution of wealth and power in the region. While most Western governments exhibit ambivalence, Moscow and China are investing heavily in building commercial infrastructure, naval capacity and military capabilities. As part of its Polar Silk Road ambitions, Beijing now actively encourages its enterprises to utilize the Northern Sea Route. Additionally, de facto control over shipping routes in the region currently rests with Moscow, which has arrogated the power to grant shipping permits—a position that American officials have already warned might contravene the UN Convention of the Law of the Seas (UNCLOS). This, however, will be the least of our concerns in the coming decade.

The collision of these geopolitical plates is not merely forcing us to reimagine our mental maps of the world. History suggests that the distribution of power will test the philosophical and institutional foundations of the world order. These continents and civilizations will soon demand a place on the high table; however, the political and cultural diversity between them is enormous. Twentieth-century templates—all of which were born as unique products of Anglo-American histories—will no longer be sufficient or reliable.

THE COLLISION OF THE REAL AND THE VIRTUAL

The collision between the virtual and the real further complicates the churn in the physical world. These once-distinct spaces are colliding with a velocity that is transforming the relationship between the individual, business, and state. At the same time, it is also disrupting the dynamics of international politics and security. Three immediate consequences have emerged as a result of this trend.

First, the aggregation of individuals in cyberspace has spawned contradictory dynamics. In a 2013 book, Jared Cohen and Eric Schmidt argued that connecting millions of individuals over an 'instantly responsive network' would have 'game-changing' implications for politics everywhere.[10] They were right about connectivity: nearly three billion individuals, around 40 per cent of the global population, now use social networks.[11] The proliferation of cheap smartphones, coupled with rapidly falling data prices, has democratized cyberspace. With millions of new individuals from Asia, Africa and Latin America getting online each year, the world will soon be networked like never before. The 'game-changing' consequences, however, appear to be extreme polarization and contestation. Digital platforms and their algorithmic processes have left individuals and communities isolated in filter bubbles and echo chambers, bereft of what democratic politics require the most—a shared sense of social realities. This is not a technological problem alone—instead, technology only amplifies the divisions that have simmered under the surface. The virtual world may have connected millions, but it has brought each of their biases, political beliefs and cultural values to the fore—with troubling consequences. Survey after survey now confirms that most democracies are deeply divided on a much wider variety of issues than ever before. In fact, a recent Pew Survey in the US found that Democrats and Republicans acknowledge that they can no longer agree on basic facts. The consequences for democracies with weaker state institutions and more fragile social cohesion are even more grim.

Second, conversations on how to manage the social, political and economic consequences of cyberspace have led to the Balkanization of infrastructure and software. States can no longer agree on how best to preserve national values in cyberspace; there is no agreement on how to regulate and govern the transformative role of technology platforms, who have taken on a sovereignty of their own; there is also no guarantee of any securing of their platforms. Increasingly, these forces are compelling the Internet to split along regional and national borders, carved up by regulatory knives. This is a phenomenon that is only likely to gain momentum. Already, authoritarian governments like China have developed the capacity to 'wall off' the Internet, using their instruments to strengthen political rule and repression. Along with Moscow, Beijing has attempted to globalize this vision of the Internet. On the other hand, even democratic actors like the EU feel compelled to re-exert their super sovereignty in an ostensible effort to protect its citizens' rights and maintain regulatory control over larger than life platforms. Meanwhile, new centres of power, like India, are concerned that they are being reduced to 'data colonies'—this term implies that their value is being extracted by extant powers. With India now considering data localization laws, it is clear that these concerns have widespread appeal.

Finally, technology has enabled conflict to operate at the societal level, cutting across commercial, political and social activity. In today's highly interdependent, networked and 'informatized' world, asymmetric military capabilities are available to even the smallest of non-state actors. The most considerable risks, however, remain state-sponsored cyber-attacks and digital influence operations. Russia's alleged attempts to interfere in the 2016 US presidential elections suggest that cyberspace is vulnerable, and has multiple entry points. Since 2016, Facebook has admitted that Russia's sophisticated Internet Research Agency bought over 3,000 Facebook and Instagram ads, which ultimately reached nearly 126 million individuals—a number that was practically the entire American electorate.[12] Businesses have not been spared from cybersecurity threats either: according to a 2017 report by the Commission on the Theft of American Intellectual Property, the US loses anywhere between $225 billion to $600 billion per year to Chinese cyber espionage tactics.[13] The US is no different: it leverages control over the largest technology platforms to enforce its writ on those it considered adversaries. Twitter, for example, has blocked several Iranian state media outlets on its platforms[14] and GitHub has banned users from Iran, Syria and Crimea.[15] With the onset of the fourth industrial revolution and its attendant technologies, these vulnerabilities are going to multiply. The individual, connected to her smartphone, networked on the Internet of Things (IoT) and reliant on AI, will be a frontline actor implicating national security.

The collision of the real and the virtual has tested one of cyberspace's most critical assumptions: that it would emerge as a global network defined by private communities. With the state making a comeback, and cyberspace looking less global than ever, 2018 may very well mark a shift in the fundamental nexus of power. Even as the economic potential of cyberspace remains profound, it is clear that social cohesion and the national security of our societies is at stake.

THE COLLISION OF TRADE AND GLOBALIZATION

The final collision is taking place over the future of globalization, the leadership of the global economy, and successful models for industrial growth and development. For one thing, it is clear that the US and its transatlantic partners appear less willing and less able to sustain and project a global market-based economy. The most immediate cause of this phenomenon is the haphazard distributional effects of globalization, with Western workers receiving the short end of the stick. Consider, for example, that the National Bureau of Economic Research (NBER) suggests that America's entry into the WTO cost as many as 2.4 million jobs between 1999 and 2011.[16] This is a story that has played out across the developed world, with McKinsey estimating that between 2005 and 2014, real incomes in developed countries fell for about 540 million individuals.[17] The citizens who were most affected by this loss in economic security were middle-class, older, white, and heavily dependent upon the manufacturing industry. In other words, this is the very same constituency that favours populist solutions and methods. In April 2016, Trump thundered that he would no longer 'surrender this country or its people to the false song of globalism'.[18] Under Trump, America is in the process of renegotiating its role in the global economy and is unwilling to shoulder the burdens of globalization.

Second, in stark contrast to Western unwillingness to promulgate the virtues of globalization, it is China that has taken the lead in defining it in the twenty-first century. This was most visible at the 2017 World Economic Forum (WEF), when Xi took centre stage in Davos and positioned China as the pallbearer of globalization. Additionally, China is employing an all-of-the-government approach to exert control over industry and using economic statecraft to maximize global power and legitimacy. The most visible manifestation of 'socialism with Chinese characteristics' is the Made in China 2025 strategy,[19] which is Beijing's state-led effort to move up the value chain from labour-intensive growth towards high tech and innovation. In the process, China is disregarding global trade rules and destroying the market share and industrial potential of other economies. If successful, the Beijing consensus, as it is often known, will mark the end of the free flow of trade, technologies, ideas and entrepreneurship. As China makes its way to a $20-trillion economy in the next decade, it will inspire a range of smaller states to adopt its own economic choices, with dangerous consequences for the global economy.

Third, the past few decades of globalization were driven by Western outreach to Eastern markets. In other words, globalization had a directional bias: Western communities paid for and designed the institutions that would manage the flow of capital and industry to emerging economies. Countries from Asia, Latin America and Africa were largely left out of this process. Today, capital is flowing from the East to the West as well, with countries like China and India searching for markets in Europe and the US. Old institutions are no longer capable of managing a bidirectional flow of globalization.

Put together, these trends have led to a loud confrontation between the US and China, the two great powers of the West and the East. The insecurity of a superpower committed to retaining its primacy in global affairs, and the spectre of rising power, with an alternative vision for global economic relations, has led to the collision of trade, finance and technology. Indeed, historians will record the year 2018 as the first year of the great Sino-American trade war. While Trump's rhetoric suggests that his motivation is bringing jobs back to the American people, his administration's strategy squarely places China's economic model in its sight. A study of the Trump administration's economic strategy makes it clear that the US is targeting the 'Made in China' initiative to choke the pipelines that have enabled China's rise over the past forty years. Both the US and China are aware that pulling ahead of the curve in innovation will translate into geopolitical power, and that this will be a winner-takes-all contest. Unsurprisingly, then, this contest is only escalating and growing in scale. It is disrupting global supply chains, long-established economic partnerships and, indeed, the foundations of the global economy.

Since the 1970s, the relocation of manufacturing processes to developing countries, especially to China, has defined global economic growth. The clash between America First and the China Dream will reshape global trade and security and will reinvigorate a debate once considered long resolved, over the 'right' political model. Increasingly, it is clear that the global economy will look very different in the twenty-first century.

RE-ORDERING THE WORLD: TOWARDS PAX SINICA

If you were an American looking out at the world in the 1990s, it would appear 'flat', much in the way Thomas Friedman described it. The Berlin Wall had fallen, Boris Yeltsin was committed to democratic capitalism, and China would soon commit to an open economic order. With the American life seeming quite universal, Francis Fukumaya's idea of 'the end of history' was looking like a reality. However, as we stand now, it has taken less than two decades for this thesis to come undone. The liberal international order is now coming to terms with its own contradictions; or, as Richard Haass quips, it is increasingly evident that this order is 'neither liberal nor worldwide nor orderly'.[20]

On the other hand, if you are a looking out at the world today from China, the picture appears far more promising. China has a strong hand to play in each of the collisions taking place. While the collective rise in the wealth of the Indo-Pacific, Eurasia and the Arctic is birthing new geopolitical actors, it is evident that China is leading the pack. Beijing is incubating new norms, entering fluid partnerships and creating new institutions to manage the emerging world order. The US and the EU are on the back foot when it comes to managing these transformations. Increasingly, the engine of connectivity in these new geographies is Chinese money, infrastructure and ambitions.

Chairman Xi has also outlined his plans to turn China into a 'cyber-superpower'. Already, China hosts the largest population with access to the Internet and is home to companies like Alibaba and Tencent, which are catching up with their Silicon Valley peers in size and value. Under Xi, China has effectively fused the gains from these developments with the Communist Party's ideology and vision, and it is creating a distinct virtual world. But Xi has grander plans. Increasingly, the world is running on Chinese applications and hardware, which covers the entire gamut of the digital economy's supply chains. Beijing will soon reap the economic, diplomatic and intelligence benefits that were once only accrued to Washington.

Finally, the Atlantic story has flown past its fly-by date. 'Democratic capitalism', it appears, has lost its sheen even in the countries that once evangelized it. In the 1990s, it was indeed a persuasive argument: the appeal of international liberalism had seen a remarkable 66 per cent rise in the number of free countries from 1988 to 1992—from forty-five to seventy-four.[21] However, China's extraordinary growth since the 1970s challenges the utility of this model. Now, more than ever, the domestic arrangements that powered the Cold War's winners appear in disarray. It is no surprise that 2018 marked both a decline in the number of identified democratic countries and the erection of significant trade barriers. Xi's China is providing a model for strong states around the world, and offering an alternative for social stability and economic growth.

These changes and collisions compel us to ask difficult questions. The emergence of new strategic geographies, the changing nature of cyberspace and the disruption of the global economy are all making it increasingly difficult to manage the global order. Pax Sinica is the Chinese salve in a world where Western thinkers appear confounded by the disorder. The lack of ideas, optimism and solutions from the Atlantic communities for the twenty-first century has made China's offering the only option for many states to embrace. Increasingly, China is the root of gifts.

IX

XI DREAMS

Located at the western edge of Tiananmen Square in the heart of Beijing, the Great Hall of the People is the place from where China shows itself to the world. The Great Hall is where the PRC government performs state functions, hosts foreign dignitaries and organizes various activities that project China's power. It is also where the National Party Congress takes place every five years. The Congress itself is about people and policy: it reviews the party's initiatives for the past term, outlines key priorities for the next five years, and appoints a new Central Committee. The nineteenth iteration of this event, held on 18 October 2017, may yet be the most important in the country's history. Since 2012, Chairman Xi had sought to transform both the party and the state: He cemented his political power through an expansive and ruthless anticorruption campaign; placed himself in key positions to influence the party, the military and the state; and extended the party's authority over every aspect of the country's governance. Xi is, without a doubt, China's most powerful leader since Mao. However, unlike Mao, who governed a poverty-stricken China, Xi commands an economy that has become a driver of global economic growth.

Xi has been instrumental in securing for China an increasingly influential position in the international community. At Davos in January 2017, Xi disavowed protectionism and championed free trade and globalization. While it is easy to dismiss this as mere rhetoric, given that China privileges the state over markets, the fact that Xi's public pronouncements stood in sharp contrast to those of President Trump merits attention. By occupying centre stage at Davos, China was telling the world that it was willing and able to occupy the mantle of global leadership, albeit with Chinese characteristics. On climate change, too, China has emerged as the most important actor—not only promising to cut down on emissions, but also investing in technologies, supply chains and markets that are critical for achieving the promises of the Paris Agreement. In Asia, the BRI is expanding Chinese influence through a series of infrastructure initiatives that Beijing claims will be the engine of the next wave of globalization and connectivity. Xi has also pursued a more nationalist foreign policy. One month after Xi took charge of the military in November 2012, Chinese aircraft encroached on Japanese airspace for the first time since 1958.[1] At the same time, the construction of artificial reefs and shoals in the South China Sea, along with the overall militarization of the region, has received top priority under Xi. Indeed, Xi appears to be stubbornly departing from Deng Xiaoping's maxim—'Observe calmly, secure our position; cope with affairs calmly; hide our capacities and bide our time; be good at maintaining a low profile; and never claim leadership.'[2]

This is why all eyes were on Xi last year, at the nineteenth National Congress of the CPC. Delivering a marathon three-and-a-half-hour speech, Xi was bullish about his country's future. 'This is a new historic juncture in China's development,' he declared, '[and the country must now] strive for the great success of socialism with Chinese characteristics for a new era, and work tirelessly to realize the Chinese Dream of national rejuvenation.'[3] Xi undoubtedly saw himself as central to this effort. Having christened himself 'core leader' in 2016—a designation previously reserved for Chairman

Mao—he inserted a new ideological guide to China's destiny: 'Xi Jinping's thought on socialism with Chinese characteristics for the new age.' This placed Xi in the pantheon of China's greatest leaders, adding to what was already a somewhat lengthy preamble, which takes 'Marxism-Leninism, Mao Zedong Thought, Deng Xiaoping Theory, Theory of the Three Represents, and the Scientific Development Outlook' as its guides to action.

A NEW EMPEROR

The nineteenth National Congress was also supposed to perform another function: that of elevating a successor. The fifteenth Party Congress in 1997, for example, named Hu Jintao and Wen Jiabao as successors to Jiang Zemin and Zhu Rongi, respectively. And Xi Jinping and Li Keqiang were elevated at the seventeenth Party Congress in 2007. Therefore, there was much anticipation, both within China and around the world, about who Xi would name as his successor at the nineteenth Congress.

He would speak no words about any succession. Less than half a year later, Xi confirmed what many had already suspected. In March 2018, China's parliament overwhelmingly voted in favour of a proposal abolishing presidential term limits—essentially making Xi the chairman of everything on an open-ended basis, and entrusting him with the great concerns of party, military and state. Of the 2,964 votes that were cast, 2,958 were in favour of the amendment, one vote was invalidated, and 'the identities of the five dissenters is—and will almost certainly remain—a mystery', as *The Guardian* put it.[4]

Again, in doing this, Xi broke from convention that had been established by Deng, who prioritized economic development and warned against 'the excessive concentration of power' of the kind China saw in the Mao era and the violence of the Cultural Revolution that followed. The reaction from global audiences was immediate: 'A new emperor' and 'president for life' were common headlines across newspapers. Even in Beijing, the signs of discontent became immediately obvious. China's censors worked overtime as soon as the news broke. An assortment of phrases such as 'constitution amendement', 're-elected', 'proclaim oneself as emperor', and 'two term limit' were erased from Weibo—China's equivalent of Twitter.[5] All references to the popular Disney character Winnie the Pooh—to whom Xi bears a resemblance, according to Weibo users—were erased as well. In some universities abroad, posters with the phrase 'Not my President' were plastered on campus walls by anonymous Chinese students.[6] Perhaps the one censored phrase that indicated both disgruntlement in China and the paranoia of the authorities was: 'I disagree.'[7] Ironically enough, the only person who seems to have praised Xi was US President Trump, who was quoted to have said 'it was great' that Xi was now president for life. 'We'll want to give that a shot someday,' he added.[8]

The key question, however, is if Chairman Xi is just another power-hungry dictator. The answer is complex. It was not truly necessary for Xi to abolish constitutional term limits for the presidency; in fact, real power rests with the Party Secretary and the Chairman of the CMC, which have no limits in the first place,[9] although still largely subject to the informal ten-year transition rule that has been in place since Zemin's regime. Instead, it would be correct to assume that Xi believes that predictability and stability are key for China's emergence as a great power. Apart from rising domestic expectations, the international climate can be far more hostile to China's growth.

At home, Xi is aware that Chinese society is undergoing a significant transition. A prosperous middle class begets new expectations, and the Party must adapt to serving new demands. The statist nature of collective leadership in the Hu Jintao era must have weighed heavily on Xi, because he now believes that what China requires is a stronger Party, with himself at its core. Simultaneously, China's economic rise and social stability must require it to play a greater role in international affairs—commensurate with its history and current heft. To achieve this, Xi will seek the erosion of the artificial borders of Asia, Europe and Africa, and intend for China to emerge as the sole arbiter of political, economic and security decisions in these regions. For India, Xi's ambitions can only mean greater rivalry. As an emerging power that harbours its own global ambitions, India cannot constrain itself to playing second fiddle.

THE PRINCIPAL CONTRADICTION

Xi has outlined the 'China Dream' explicitly: A 'moderately well-off society' by 2021 and a 'democratic, civilized, harmonious, and modern socialist country' by 2049.[10] Central to achieving this vision is what the Chinese understand as resolving the 'principal contradictions' of a state. By identifying and resolving these contradictions, society is able to develop peacefully. This line of thinking formed the crux of Mao's influential 1937 essay, 'On Contradictions', where he identified an irreconcilable class war between the proletariat and the bourgeoisie as the two opposing social forces.[11] Intent on preventing the horrors of the Cultural Revolution that followed from this thought, as well as on generating wealth, Deng Xiaoping described the principal contradiction in 1981 as the one between 'the ever-growing material and cultural needs of the people and backward social production'.[12] By framing the problem in this manner, Chinese leaders could justify market reforms and reconcile the tenets of socialism with those of a market economy, thus giving birth to what would be known as 'socialism with Chinese characteristics'.

Nearly four decades later, the results are clear enough: With a Gross Domestic Product (GDP) of $11.2 trillion, China is today the world's second-largest economy and continues to climb up the industrial value chain;[13] it is ranked twenty-second on the Global Innovation index;[14] by 2014, China was trading nearly $4.3 trillion of goods and services, making it the world's largest trading nation;[15] and it now boasts one of the world's most advanced militaries, allotting nearly $175 billion to the forces' modernization in 2018.[16] This trailblazing economic growth, however, has come with social costs, such as huge inequity: As China boasts over a million millionaires, the richest 1 per cent of households own one-third of the country's wealth.[17] Urbanization is also taking its toll: nearly 200 million rural migrants travel across China in search of factory jobs that offer poor pay and hazardous working conditions; and many of China's major cities, most prominently Beijing, are enveloped in dense smog for many months of the year. There is also the problem of corruption, with Transparency International's Corruption Perceptions Index (CPI) ranking China seventy-seventh out of 180 countries.[18]

A survey by the Pew Research Center in 2015 showed that the Chinese people viewed corruption, pollution, and inequality as their country's most pressing problems.[19] Unsurprisingly, then, Xi has reframed the principal contradiction as the tension between 'unbalanced and inadequate development' and the 'people's ever-growing needs for a better life'. This includes, in Xi's words, 'demands for democracy, the rule of law, fairness and justice, security, and a better environment'. This is the crux of the 'New Era' that Chairman Xi promises. In essence, he recognizes that economic growth alone is not enough; rather, the party must embrace 'well-rounded human development and all-round social progress'.

While the idea of solving contradictions itself is ambiguous, the importance of this framework for both the direction of the state, and Xi's own personal ambitions, are momentous. What Xi is saying is that he alone can provide what China's increasingly ambitious middle class expects: clean governance, efficient provision of government services such as education and healthcare, affordable housing, and a cleaner environment. The text of his report at the nineteenth Party Congress is a key indicator of his intentions: the phrases 'rural rejuvenation', 'ecology', and 'environment' were mentioned more times than 'market' or 'economy'.[20] It is unsurprising, then, that Xi, who *The Economist* called 'the world's most powerful man',[21] spent the better part of 2017 talking about toilets, describing them as a 'concrete part of advancing our country's revitalization'.[22]

This restatement of the Chinese society's principal contradiction will have enormous implications: It signals Xi's personal ambition of being the president that will turn China from a poor middle-class country to a prosperous society that forms the backbone of a new great power. It also validates the criticism of former Premier Wen Jiabao, who warned in 2007 that the Chinese economy was increasingly becoming 'unstable, unbalanced, uncoordinated, and [ultimately] unsustainable'.[23] Many believe that Xi now has the power and authority to correct this; according to Moody's, Xi's consolidation of power 'could advance the process of economic reform and rebalancing, because one obstacle to reform has been the misalignment of incentives between the central leadership and other officials'.[24] Deng, who was the principal architect of China's economic reforms beginning in the late 1970s, saw 'the separation of the party and government' as key towards rejuvenating the economy. Chairman Xi sees things differently. In an allusion to Chairman Mao, he had once said: 'Party, government, military, society and education, east, west, south, north, the Party governs everything.'[25]

COLLECTIVE LEADERSHIP TO COMPLETE CONTROL

Xi now faces the enormous challenge of making the right choices for China's economy. In 2013, Xi promised to give the market a 'decisive role' in the economy. Since then, it is apparent that Xi has done with the economy what he has done with the rest of China: elevated the role and power of the Communist Party. As the goal of doubling the 2010 GDP of China by 2020 remains a policy priority, Xi has called on the 'national champions'—or state-owned enterprises of China—to fulfil this role. Xi has also mandated the presence of Party members in almost every commercial venture in China, giving them key management and investment decision-making powers. Moreover, its action plan for what it calls 'Made in China 2025' puts to rest any notion that the country might now be looking at liberalizing its economy. The plan envisions China emerging as the industry leader on high-technology manufacturing and advance technologies such as robotics, AI, and genomics. It seeks to indigenize and relocate global supply chains to the Chinese mainland with generous support from the Party in the form of easy credit, domestic procurement clauses, and trade barriers. For now, Xi has made it clear that any real market reform that would reduce the Party's influence is undesirable.

This is hardly surprising. Whenever he speaks at home, he extols absolute loyalty to the Party. The Party itself under Xi, however, has undergone a massive transformation. Since at least the 1990s, the PRC has embraced the idea of 'collective leadership'. In 2007, a communique issued by the Party Congress stated that collective leadership is 'a system with a division of responsibilities among individual leaders in an effort to prevent arbitrary decision-making by a single top leader'.[26] Various analysts have said that the pillars of China's 'authoritarian resilience' were intra-party democracy, merit-based recruitment, delegation of power and consultative decision-making. Deng Xiaoping himself once argued that collective leadership was key to China's stability.[27] Under Hu Jintao, however, this principle was severely tested. During a period referred to as 'the lost decade', Chinese society was marred by corruption and social unrest; it was when Chinese politics was at its factional worst, torn between the elitist group who 'generally represented the interests of entrepreneurs and the coastal region', and populists who 'represent[ed] the interests of the labouring classes and the inland region'.[28] At the same time, the same decentralization that characterized the Deng era came to represent a disconnect between Beijing and local officials in the provinces—a divide captured aptly by the Chinese proverb: 'The mountains are high and the emperor is far away.'[29]

Perhaps aware of this reality, Xi has eroded this consensus.

According to a Party source interviewed by the *Nikkei Asian Review* in early 2018, 'Xi is now aiming to be free of China's collective leadership system. His ideal is to have strong powers similar to those granted to a US president.'[30] The complete centralization of power under Xi bears testament to this desire: not only is he President, general secretary of the Party, and Chairman of the CMC, but Xi also chairs the Central Leading Group for Comprehensively Deepening Reforms as well as the National Security Commission—two of the most important decision-making bodies in China. Simultaneously, he chairs several leading groups on Internet governance, military reform, and foreign affairs, among other aspects of governance. Many of these leading groups are also staffed by Party officials who worked with him during his younger days in provinces such as Zhejiang and Fujian—in other words, their loyalty is beyond question.[31]

What surprised many was Xi's absolute control over the PLA. Writing for *The Wall Street Journal*, Andrew Erickson notes that Xi's 'ability to impose his will on the PLA…is a skill that his predecessor Hu Jintao lacked utterly and that Jiang Zemin wielded inconsistently'.[32] During a high-profile address to Chinese troops stationed in Hong Kong to mark the twentieth anniversary of the British handover, Xi reportedly asked them to refer to him as 'Chairman'—a break from the conventional 'leader' that troops otherwise used, and a powerful indication of his domestic strength and complete control over China.[33]

At the heart of Xi's so-called new era for both society and industry, then, appears to be more centralized Party control. Indeed, it does not seem likely that the intimidation of human rights activists, dissenters and religious minorities will subside. At the same time, Xi will preside over the creation of the Orwellian social credit system, which will track citizens' behaviour in astonishingly granular detail using AI, Big Data, and the IoT. As Elizabeth Economy writes in her new book, *The Third Revolution,* Xi's call for the 'rejuvenation of the Chinese nation' is not entirely novel.

Both Hu Jintao and Deng Xiaoping have in one way or another called for the 'invigoration' of China. Xi, however, is intent on reform without opening up.[34] It is this new framework that will guide China's political economy. Over the past decade, Beijing has attempted to enact several reforms that will address its persistent domestic imbalances. Ultimately, Xi's power grab alters the political ecosystem within which they will operate. This system is party first, with core leader Xi at the helm.

EVERYTHING UNDER THE HEAVENS

Of course, China's economic rise and stability will have major implications on how it reshapes the world order. The great rejuvenation of China—Xi's nationalist calling card—is an appeal to the country's historical place in world affairs. Ever since China's last imperial dynasty was defeated by the British Navy in the mid-nineteenth century, the quest for wealth, power and international prestige has preoccupied China's elites. Indeed, *Xinhua* notes, 'By 2050, two centuries after the Opium Wars, which plunged the "Middle Kingdom" into a period of hurt and shame, China is set to regain its might and re-ascend to the top of the world.'[35] The sheer number of foreign trips that Xi has taken since becoming President is a testament to this belief: Nearly twenty-eight, covering fifty-six countries across five continents—the highest number for any Chinese leader.[36] Xi is aware that China's global power ambitions could not have come at a better time. Indeed, the nineteenth Party Congress report notes that '...relative international forces are becoming more balanced'.

This was a slightly nuanced recognition of the perception that Western powers were unable to anchor the post-World War II international order. The US and the EU have both faced a succession of economic and social troubles over the past several years. For the first time since the end of the Cold War, an American president is speaking of economic protectionism, disavowing multilateral diplomacy and demanding more from military alliances. The EU, on the other hand, has been gripped by a crisis of identity, as an inflexible Brussels struggles to manage economic inequality while integrating the millions of migrants from the Middle East, thus putting to test the values of multiculturalism and liberalism that defined post-war Europe. This turmoil has left a leadership vacuum in terms of the global economy, epochal ecological change and collective security. It is in this vacuum that Chairman Xi sees opportunity: By the middle of the twenty-first century, Xi boasts, China will have become a global leader in terms of comprehensive national power and international influence.

Yet, by any measure, China *is* already a global power. As we have discussed before, during Xi's 2012 visit to Washington, D.C. as vice president, Xi called for a 'new type of great power relations' between the US and China. Elizabeth Economy writes that such ambitions reflect Xi's confidence that China is in a position to shape the international order—or capable of 'constructing international playgrounds' and 'creating the rules' of the game, as he would later say in a speech in 2014.[37] China's ambition, as journalist Howard French notes, is deeply historical. 'For the better part of two millennia,' writes French, 'the norm for China, from its own perspective, was a natural dominion over everything under the heaven, a concept known in the Chinese language as *tian xia*.'[38] Xi has been masterful in his employment of history to stoke nationalism among his people. 'Only by having a correct recognition of history,' he once said, 'can it be possible for us to open up a better future. Forgetting history signifies betrayal.'[39]

The first major flashpoints of this invigorated nationalism are likely to be the SCS, where steady progress in the construction of islands and reefs has been highlighted as a major achievement by Xi; and Taiwan, which Xi claims must be reunited with the mainland to achieve the great rejuvenation of the Chinese nation. This is another key reason for Xi to remain in power. Since 2012, he has reformed and rationalized personnel management, reorganized the military into 'theatre commands', created new units to develop and deploy advanced technologies, and promoted a younger generation of military elite.[40] However, these upheavals have created certain efficiency problems, including the dislocation of units, anxiety amongst senior officers and unfamiliar organizational structures.[41] Xi intends to power through these reforms and oversee a streamlined military that will achieve full modernization by 2035. He wants to ensure that the PLA becomes a global top-tier fighting force capable of winning wars by the mid-century. In the SCS, China has adopted a strategy of 'active defence'—otherwise referred to as anti-access/area denial (A2/AD), which involves utilizing long-range precision missiles, active control over contested waters, and denial of navigation to preclude American intervention in the region.

Taking note of this, US Admiral Harry Harris has already called Beijing's militarization of the SCS 'a coordinated, methodical and strategic' attempt to 'erode the free and open international order'; he warned that 'China's impressive military build-up could soon challenge the US across almost every domain'.[42] Further, the US National Security Strategy (NSS) now refers to China as a 'revisionist power', and the US Senate passed the Taiwan Travel Act in 2018, clarifying that it 'should be US policy' to allow American and Taiwanese officials to meet for high-level talks.[43] On 16 April 2018, Xi sent a clear message to the US and the world by ordering live fire drills in the Taiwan Strait, only days after he presided over a large-scale naval display in the SCS that involved 'more than 10,000 naval officers, seventy-six fighter jets, and a flotilla of forty-eight warships and submarines'.[44]

Nearly three years ago, Graham Allison wrote that when a rising power confronts an incumbent superpower, war ensues.[45] He titled the book *Thucydides Trap* in memory of the Athenian historian, who analysed this dynamic between Athens and Sparta nearly 2,400 years ago. Whether or not the Thucydides trap plays out in the SCS region may be uncertain, but the signs are ominous.

The real concern, however, is China's BRI. This dense network of infrastructure projects, energy lines, supply chains and trade routes intends to erode the artificial political geography of Asia and Europe. Again, Xi has been masterful in employing history to court support for the BRI: 'More than 2,100 years ago,' he said, 'during the Han Dynasty a Chinese envoy named Zhang Qian was twice sent to Central Asia,' and these journeys would 'start the Silk Road linking the East and West, Asia and Europe.'[46] From railway lines in Southeast Asia, to the comprehensive CPEC in Central Asia, to a military base in Djibouti, Africa, and onwards to the Greek port of Piraeus—Xi has staked his legacy on being able to integrate Asia, Africa and Europe into one overarching political, economic and military architecture, with Beijing as its central node. Foreign minister Wang called it '... [The] largest international cooperation platform in the world and the most popular international public product.'[47]

The word 'co-operation', however, is often loosely thrown about by Chinese officials. A recent review of eight countries that have signed on to the BRI revealed what countries like India already knew: the projects are financially unsustainable, the trade imbalance with Beijing is too high, environmental costs are ballooning and strategic assets are being collateralised for debt.[48] When asked why Sri Lanka had handed over the strategically located Hambantota port to China for a ninety-nine-year lease, Mahinda Samarasinghe, Sri Lanka's Minister of Ports and Shipping, answered woefully: 'We had to take a decision to get out of this debt trap.'[49]

China is now wary that a counter-mobilization of other regional powers is taking place against the BRI. Beginning with a speech by former US Secretary of State Rex Tillerson in October 2017, who criticized the BRI for its 'predatory economics',[50] like-minded 'Indo-Pacific' democracies have begun to align their normative interests, economic statecraft and military postures to prevent Beijing from unilaterally shaping Asia's governance architecture. While the US, Japan, India and Australia all have their own axe to grind with China for various political and military reasons, they are well aware that faulty economics could be the Achilles' heel of the

BRI. The signs of discontent are already apparent in many parts of the world—protests against Chinese investments have erupted from Kazakhstan in Central Asia to Kenya in Africa, Bangladesh and Sri Lanka in South Asia, and in parts of Southeast Asia as well. Accordingly, members of the renewed Quadrilateral Initiative (i.e., India, Japan, Australia, the US) are creating new synergies in their economic statecraft: The US's free and open Indo-Pacific strategy, the Indo-Japan Act East Forum and the new Asia-Africa Growth Corridor (AAGC). In each case, these states are raising capital to meet the connectivity requirements of developing countries and pushing for better qualitative economic frameworks and transparent investment standards.

To address these concerns, Xi is placing his bets on a new agency for international development that was tasked with overseeing China's 'major country' (economic) diplomacy.[51] This new agency is significant as it indicates that Beijing is aware that it must create a more equitable economic framework to manage its investments and quell the discontent in target regions. However, Beijing's major country diplomacy, at least when it comes to those states that are hesitant about the BRI, often involves coercion. For the most part, Southeast Asia has had to bear the brunt of China's heft. China has used its loose purse strings to effectively divide and rule the ASEAN. Despite having suffered the worst of Beijing's land reclamation policies in the SCS, for example, Rodrigo Duterte of the Philippines is confident that he can come to an arrangement with China—a view undoubtedly buttressed by nearly $24 billion in investment proposals promised by China.[52] For the same reasons, successive ASEAN communiques have failed to explicitly highlight Beijing's militarization of the SCS. Not that this behaviour is limited to Asia: in 2016, both Hungary and Greece—major beneficiaries of Chinese investments—refused to adopt a EU statement on the SCS, and fought hard to prevent any major overhaul of investment policies that would limit Beijing's financial offerings.[53] This, in fact, is a key overarching objective of the BRI—to erode the autonomous politics of various sub-regions around the world through economic statecraft, military coercion, or both. Only by ensuring that regional blocs do not cohesively act as one unit can the BRI succeed. Xi has staked his personal legacy on this.

The BRI is also important to China because it ultimately paves the way for Xi's institutional statecraft. Xi wants China to emerge as the next driver of globalization—however, he wants to do this in a manner that is distinct from the 'Washington consensus', which was based on transparent free markets. In its place, Xi will sell 'socialism with Chinese characteristics'—a unique blend of state control over industry and capitalism, or what India's former foreign secretary calls 'non-market economics'.[54] Today's global institutions, such as the World Bank, are dominated by America's economic model—and China seeks to supplant these institutions with those that support the 'Beijing consensus', such as the BRICS NDB, the RCEP trade agreement, and the AIIB. China is even setting up new 'international tribunals' to manage trade and investment disputes arising from the BRI. However, it is unclear what standards of dispute settlement will be employed, and which law will be given precedence. The most obvious implication of this new institution is to prevent disputes involving the BRI from being settled under the legal system of potential competitors. Ultimately, these institutions bolster Beijing's influence in recipient countries; give China leverage over other multilateral institutions; and enhance Beijing's global leadership status. If China succeeds in this endeavour, it will fundamentally alter the nature of global relations. For nearly seventy years, the combination of political liberalism and economic free markets succeeded in the global marketplace of ideas. As Wang Yi states, '...the most essential and meaningful results of China's diplomacy as a major country with Chinese characteristics' is that China can now 'provide a new path for all developing countries to modernization'.[55]

As Elizabeth Economy states bluntly: 'China is essentially, an illiberal country claiming leadership in a liberal international order'[56]—another contradiction it undoubtedly seeks to resolve.

And it has found a willing partner in Moscow. In 2016, former Chinese vice-foreign minister Fu Ying wrote in *Foreign Affairs* that it would be incorrect to characterize the Sino-Russian relationship as one that is a 'marriage of convenience'; instead, she writes, 'changes in international relations since the end of the Cold War have only brought the two countries closer together'.[57] The official was essentially blaming Washington's unilateralisms for bringing them together. Today, both Moscow and Beijing remain convinced that the centre of gravity in international politics is drifting from the Atlantic to the Eurasian system—a geography they are both particularly well placed to influence. While ideologically and economically whittling away at the EU—through Russian support for far-right parties and China's financial offerings—both these countries have enhanced economic cooperation through interaction between the BRI and the Eurasia Economic Union (EEAU), and are coordinating security and governance policy under the SCO. At the same time, both countries have often taken similar positions at the UN, such as on the Syria crisis, and have stepped up military exercises in disputed areas such as the SCS. Russia is merely China's most influential partner in what is otherwise a concerted effort to build a coalition of states who are no longer willing to subscribe to the notion that domestic development and global governance is only achievable under the conditions of democracy and free markets.

In 1949, Mao achieved the goal of independence; in the 1980s, Deng set China on a path that would make it wealthy; and Xi believes that the time has now come to build a community with a shared destiny for mankind and fulfil the objective of ensuring that China will continue to play its part as a major and responsible country, take an active part in reforming and developing the global governance system, and keep contributing Chinese wisdom and strength to global governance. Whether or not Xi will say so explicitly, he intends to attempt what no modern Chinese leader has accomplished: the revival of the ancient Chinese system of *Tian xia*—a worldview as old as the Han Dynasty, that places China at the apex of a network of political, cultural, economic and military regimes—or as Xi notes, 'ever closer to centre stage in global affairs'.

From the Himalayas to the High Seas

To be sure, there are several irritants to Xi's ambitions—and none more persistent than India. During the last five years under Xi, tensions between the two countries have only exacerbated. For example, China has repeatedly blocked efforts at the UN to list Pakistan-based Masood Azhar, mastermind of the recent Pathankot attack in India, as a 'global terrorist'. In June 2016, China vetoed India's bid to become a full-fledged member of the Nuclear Suppliers Group (NSG). In April 2015, Beijing announced the CPEC, which passes through Pakistan Occupied Kashmir (PoK). China has also steadily increased its presence in India's neighbourhood, both economically—through BRI projects in Bangladesh, Nepal, Bhutan, Sri Lanka and Afghanistan—as well as strategically, by increasing the number of military deployments in the IOR.

Understanding the reasons are not that difficult: India and China are now structurally set to collide. They are the world's largest democracy and autocracy, respectively; they are expected to become two of the three largest economies in the coming decades; they are home to a few million of the world's millionaires, and hundreds of millions of the world's poor; they host two of the largest militaries in the world and have two of the highest defence expenditures; and, most importantly, each of them harbours ambitions of becoming a global leader. Indeed, the wealth and power of the world is inextricably moving eastwards towards Asia. India and China are in a race to define the contours of this region's governance.

If China likes thinking of the world in contradictions, then it only needs to look at its relationship with India. The fundamental contradiction is how each nation views its role in Asia. Just like for China, India's rapid economic rise will reshape the global balance of power in the coming decades. Unlike China, however, India is defined by a vibrant democratic political system, and an economy that largely relies on private-sector entrepreneurial dynamism. Indeed, at the World Economic Forum in 2018, Prime Minister Modi made it clear that India's democracy is 'a force for stability' in an otherwise global state of uncertainty and flux.[58] Just as China employs history in defining its relationships, India believes that 'Asia's re-emergence is the greatest phenomenon of our era'—as Modi declared at the thirty-seventh Singapore lecture in late 2015. India's reintegration with a broader Asia, he said, was a 'return to history', announcing that India is 'retracing our ancient maritime and land routes, with the natural instincts of an ancient relationship'.[59] China understands that if India can succeed in lifting millions of its people out of poverty, and emerges as a new engine of global economic growth, it will provide an alternative development model to the developing world—one that is completely different from Beijing's preferences and equally attractive.

Perhaps the most obvious indication that India and China are on a collision course is New Delhi's opposition to the BRI. India has always been reluctant to remain a 'passive recipient of outcomes', as former foreign secretary Jaishankar said.[60] Following Modi's state visit to Beijing in May 2015, where New Delhi expressed irritation that it was not privy to conversations on the OBOR initiative (as it was known then), India has emerged as a forthright critic of the BRI, calling it Beijing's attempt to 'hardwire influence' in Asia.[61] At the same time, India is also ramping up its own connectivity projects, such as the India–Myanmar–Thailand Trilateral Highway, the Chabahar Port in Iran, and the International North South Transportation Corridor (INSTC) with Russia. Further, India is partnering with Japan to launch the AAGC, which seeks to propel growth, investment and connectivity between the two regions. Similarly, in December 2017, India hosted the ASEAN–India Connectivity Summit (AICS) in a bid to offer alternatives to Chinese investments in the region. In terms of geography, these projects seek to connect the Indian Ocean, the Persian Gulf and Europe—almost exactly the regions that the BRI will target. However, India is decidedly a different power. By articulating its own norms, and aligning with like-minded partners under the Quadrilateral Dialogue, India is making it clear that it will not rely on predatory economics, and will, instead, attempt to foster a rules-based order that ensures financial sustainability and good governance in relation to connectivity initiatives.

Under Xi's command, such disputes over economic relations and global leadership have also spilt over into military conflicts that now extends from the 'Himalayas to the high seas'. Despite the fact that the Doklam standoff had ostensibly come to an end in August 2017 following a 'mutual withdrawal' ahead of a BRICS summit a month later, Chinese forces remain in the region and do not appear ready to withdraw yet. In a series of reports for *The Print* that have caused embarrassment to New Delhi, retired Colonel Vinayak Bhat has used satellite imagery to detail the build-up of PLA forces in and around Doklam, including helipads, concrete fighting posts, and new trenches.[62] China's foreign affairs spokesperson, in fact made it clear that China would 'continue with its exercise of sovereign rights' in the disputed area.[63]

At the same time, Maldives President Abdulla Yameen has declared a state of emergency in a country that is traditionally considered part of 'India's backyard', and has refused to yield to calls from the international community, including India, to restore democracy. His only friend so far has been China—and understandably so. Beijing has invested nearly $1 billion in investment projects in the island state; has obtained the lease of the 'uninhabited island Feydhoo Finolhu for tourism use for fifty years'; and is now Male's largest creditor, accounting for nearly 70 per cent of the state's debt.[64] Ominously, even as the tropical island was in a state of emergency and India's next moves were yet undecided, eleven Chinese warships sailed into the East Indian Ocean early this year in what was undoubtedly a form of soft signalling to New Delhi.[65] In a story that is now familiar across the South Asian subcontinent, China's hard economic power, coupled with its rising military profile, is eclipsing India's historical civilizational ties and its recent commercial outreach.

To quell some of these tensions, Modi and Xi met for an 'informal summit' at Wuhan in April 2018. Coming ahead of Modi's visit to China for the SCO Summit in June later that year, expectations were uncertain about the two-day meeting that would see both leaders 'walk by a lake, visit museums, and even take a boat ride'.[66] The first sign of this rapprochement was foreign secretary Vijay Keshav Gokhale's note to the Cabinet Secretary that senior leaders from the government must not attend a public event organized by Tibetan leaders to thank India for hosting them for nearly fifty years and counting.[67] That same month, India reportedly informed their Chinese counterparts that it would not intervene in the Maldives, and that it expected China to reciprocate this measure of 'strategic trust' by not crossing certain 'lines of legitimacy'.[68] Chinese foreign minister Wang Yi, for his part, has resorted to clichés, suggesting that 'the Chinese dragon and the Indian elephant must not fight each other but dance with each other'.[69]

The results, ultimately, were underwhelming: Apart from calls to accelerate economic cooperation, and the possibility of exploring joint development partnerships in Afghanistan, neither country could agree on key bilateral irritants, such as the BRI, Pakistan, or Indo-Pacific security. Rather than the results of the summit itself, the analysis around it gave far more illumination. Some believe that the summit was a product of 'Asia's imbalance of power'—a weaker India seeking reprieve from a domineering Beijing.[70] Others believed that 'Trump is driving Xi into Modi's arms'—alluding to global economic tensions that have arisen as a result of Trump's trade posture against China, and its consequent search for alternative partners.[71] In truth, both from India's and China's side, the overtures are temporary: New Delhi was gearing up for national elections in 2019, and Beijing is in the midst of a potentially costly 'trade war' with the US—and neither of them is keen to manage another flashpoint.

Prior to the visit, Modi tweeted in April that he would be

visiting Xi to 'discuss our respective visions and priorities for national development, particularly in the context of [the] current and future international situation'.[72] Unfortunately, the fact remains that these visions are at odds with each other. In the long run, the India-China relationship runs on multiple fault lines—civilizational, historical, economic and military—and Xi Jinping intends to tip the scales in favour of China before India can catch up. The central problem is that Beijing refuses to recognize India's influence, power or prerogatives, in its own neighbourhood and in the extended region. From claiming that India behaves as a hegemon in its region to telling New Delhi that the Indian Ocean does not belong to India, Beijing is repeatedly dismissive of India's great-power ambitions. The military and economic disparity between the two countries only bolsters Beijing's confidence. Indians are acutely aware of this reality—in 2017, a survey by the Pew Research Center found that only 21 per cent of Indians surveyed had confidence in Chinese President Xi Jinping to 'do the right thing'.[73] As China's immediate neighbour, and a diverse and chaotic democracy with its own global ambitions, India is facing the obvious implications of Xi's extended presidency: greater turbulence in the near future.

THE PARADOX OF POWER

Clearly, the import of Xi's power grab is enormous. In a world that is 'in the midst of profound and complex changes', as the nineteenth Party Congress report notes, Xi now enjoys political stability to oversee China's rise as a global power, and by extension, emerge as the greatest Chinese leader in modern history. He must deal with a hostile US, while managing complex social, economic and ecological problems at home. His decision to remain Party President past 2023 only serves to show that Xi believes in his own ability to steer China through these headwinds. For political systems with shorter timelines and democratic constraints, this is an impossible task. For Xi, it is within reach.

At home, it remains to be seen whether or not Xi can fundamentally alter China's social contract. A larger, more prosperous and more technology-savvy middle class will place new types of pressure on China's governance system. If Xi can successfully deliver on his 'better life' agenda, he will truly have a new model for development. China will become the first high-income autocracy, an achievement many considered impossible. This will have tremendous spillover effects in the international system. Already, Xi has made it clear that the revival of the Middle Kingdom will be accompanied by the redrawing of geographical borders, a transformation of the global institutional landscape and the death of diversity in China's periphery. If Beijing can provide an alternative to liberal democracy, the normative foundations of the international liberal order will be put under considerable stress.

For emerging democracies such as India, this is a fundamental challenge. Competition with China will not merely be geographical or economical, but ultimately ideological too—India must not only provide a bulwark against Beijing's militarization, but should now prove to developing countries in Asia and Africa that liberal democracy is a fundamentally more utilitarian political model.

However, Xi must solve a paradox for himself. Without having a clear map for political succession, Xi risks facing the ire of not only China's ordinary citizens if he fails to deliver on his promises, but also the disenfranchised Chinese elites—of which there are many, given his anticorruption programme and consolidation of power. Indeed, under Xi, expenditure on domestic security has increased exponentially, touching nearly $200 billion in 2017 alone[74]—in what is perhaps an indication that he is concerned about unrest at home.

On the international front, Xi's renewed nationalism and assertiveness is facing resistance from a variety of fronts. As the implications of investments under the BRI become more apparent, developing states are becoming increasingly wary about political pressure from Beijing; if the economic premise behind these investments begin failing, Chinese firms have the most to lose. At the same time, the US is now preparing for great-power rivalry with China—breaking from nearly two decades of doctrinal emphasis on terrorism as the primary threat to American security. Both the US's NSS 2017 and the National Defence Strategy 2018 have singled out China (along with Russia) as 'revisionist powers', claiming that they seek to 'shape a world consistent with their authoritarian model—gaining veto authority over other nations' economic, diplomatic, and security decisions'.[75] In tandem, regional powers such as India, Japan and Australia are curtailing Beijing's ability to act unilaterally, and are creating networks of partnerships that will increasingly coalesce with the objective of preventing the rise of a China-led order in Asia.

For now, Xi remains popular with the Chinese masses, and increasingly the most important actor in the international system. However, while autocratic politics may deliver some economic benefits and consistency in international relations, sans any checks and balances, the threat of overreach, conflict or collapse remains persistent. What tends to follow the collapse of these systems is a period of turmoil and conflict—something China and the world cannot afford.

EPILOGUE

THE ASIAN CENTURY AND THE INDO-PACIFIC: MANOEUVRING BETWEEN CAMARADERIE AND CONTEST

To understand India-China relations during the first tenure of Prime Minister Modi, it is vital to keep in mind the broader rubric of rapidly changing political forces in Asia. Over the past two decades, the Asian Century has been defined by the rise of China, and to a lesser extent, India's economic growth. It has also been characterized by cooperation between the two Asian giants in a number of forums, such as the BRICS, and more recently at the NDB and AIIB. Even though their shared border has remained a point of friction, China and India have often found themselves defending similar positions in global arenas on issues such as trade and climate change.

This quasi-camaraderie ended in 2012 when Chairman Xi proclaimed that the Middle Kingdom was committed to realizing the China Dream by mid-century. Since then, Beijing has attempted to globalize its own 'internal arrangement', organizing societies based on a mix of political authoritarianism and state-led capitalism. In 2017, Chairman Xi called this 'Socialism with Chinese characteristics for a New Era' and offered it to the world to embrace.

These developments marked an important point of departure between China and India. Beijing was now visibly willing to dictate the political, economic, and security architecture of the larger Asian continent. In doing so, it had little respect for existing sub-regional groups and balance of power arrangements such as those in Central, South, and Southeast Asia, extending right up to the EU. The BRI, which seeks to alter existing political geographies and economic models, is China's most potent tool in this regard.

China's expansive geopolitical ambition has naturally given rise to opposition from others. As a self-described leading power, India was the first to vocalize discontent with the BRI and thereby set the template for the other critics that have emerged. From this growing global pushback against China's geopolitical ambitions, a new conceptualization for Asia has emerged: the Indo-Pacific. While this was initially an American construct, India is undoubtedly one of the lynchpins of this new geography. The framing of this political geography is different from the imagined Asian century. The Indo-Pacific construct is driven by contest, conflict and competition, along with some cooperation to mitigate these adverse developments.

This trend of vacillation between camaraderie in the Asian century to the contest and acrimony in the Indo-Pacific has defined the past five years of the India-China bilateral relationship. Consider, for example, the political dynamics of the China-led AIIB. India is the second-largest shareholder in this institution, which was widely recognized as emblematic of Asia's rise and America's diminished influence over the international economic order. It was also perhaps the strongest indicator of cooperation between India and China. Contrast this with the BRI. China is coopting states in the Indo-Pacific into its broader BRI network to serve its export and national security interests, while disregarding the territorial integrity of India and ignoring India's priorities and vision for Asia.

Similarly, consider India's ascension into the SCO. The SCO has developed norms that serve as a direct counterpoint to the existing liberal international order. It is an impressive testament to how multipolarity has given rise to new engagements and propositions. From cyberspace to multilateral trade, the organization, led by Beijing, is developing uniquely Asian solutions to political, economic and security imperatives. In 2017, India joined other members to criticize the US' aggressive attitude to trade. On the other hand, India is also invested in the revival of the Quadrilateral Initiative, a grouping of democracies in the Indo-Pacific. The Quad seeks to preserve a democratic and rules-based order in the region. As in the SCO, cooperation is multifaceted and encompasses infrastructure investment, cyber norms, and maritime security cooperation. As part of the revived Quad, India seeks to respond to China's mercantilist trade and investment propositions and its maritime coercion.

Clearly, two contradictory forces drive the bilateral today—the appeal of an Asian century that seeks to escape the burden of colonialism, and a contest in the Indo-Pacific to avoid a new form of subjugation. This dynamic was invariably going to produce new frictions, and ultimately culminated in a skirmish in the Himalayas. The Doklam standoff in the summer of 2017 marked the nadir of Indio-China relations and the sharpest decline in bilateral relations between the two powers in over four decades. Fundamentally, the dispute represented a struggle to define and then manage Asia. The standoff will likely be remembered as a moment when a sovereign finally stood up to China's aggressive attempts to redraw political maps. Beijing is unlikely to either forget or forgive this. It will be naïve to ignore the acrimony, unease, contest, and struggle that has defined the relationship between the two countries ever since.

Politically, China has attempted to choke India's options. Beijing was not being petty when it refused to allow Masood Azhar's listing as a global terrorist, or when it objected to the Dalai Lama's travelling in India, or when it refused to accept India into the NSG. It was being unrelentingly strategic in undermining India's capacity to influence global and regional political developments through these actions.

On the economic front, the numbers tell an obvious story about how China views the relationship with India: India is merely a market for Chinese-manufactured industrial and consumer goods. China's mercantilism offers no room for partnership, only dependence. Despite multiple negotiations in which India has indicated its displeasure with the negative balance of trade, the difference has only grown.

On the security front, Beijing has completely disregarded India's concerns in Kashmir by investing in the CPEC. It has also attempted to undermine India's influence in its neighbourhood, most dramatically in the Maldives, Nepal, and Sri Lanka, even as it has sustained its overtures to Bangladesh. The Middle Kingdom has also been unrelenting in its pressure around Doklam, with satellite imagery suggesting that it maintain a growing security presence in the region.

By exercising diplomatic, economic, and military pressure on India within the region, China is positioning itself to design Asia's security and political architecture unilaterally. This vision is at odds with the original conceptualization of the Asian century, which was fundamentally a story of the rise of a group of countries in the region. Indeed, twenty-first-century Asia will not be defined by developing countries acting in solidarity while being led by China and India. Instead, it will be defined by Beijing's attempt to integrate, on its own terms and for its own interests, the Eurasian landmass.

Before India can respond to China with its own propositions, it must acknowledge another set of contradictory forces that drive the relationship. Even while China may apply tremendous pressure on the political and security front, it has emerged as the largest investor in key areas that are likely to drive India's economic growth. As India's economy moves towards the \$5-trillion mark, both political friction and economic engagement with China will only increase. In managing this, India will find little help from the

North-Atlantic countries—who are themselves struggling to set the terms of engagement with China, both individually and collectively. Italy's decision to join the BRI and the EU's inability to decide on the future of 5G infrastructure only drive home this point.

India will have to build its own capacity to resist and counteract China's political aggression, even as it embraces investments and commercial opportunities. This is certainly easier said than done. However, China, through its own emergence, has demonstrated the way to do this. For years, it has benefited from the American economy and its investments even as it has pushed back against a US-led world order and its presence in the Western Pacific. This is a template that India must emulate. This will be Prime Minister Modi's most complex task in his second term—navigating the disconnect between the opportunities of the Asian century and the hard realities of the Indo-Pacific.

INDIA'S ROLE IN A POST-WESTERN LIBERAL ORDER

How, then, is India to successfully navigate its relationship with China and its role as a leader in Asia at large? At first blush, the facts may lead readers to believe that Chinese leadership, or worse, hegemony, is inevitable. Counterintuitively, however, it is in the wake of Pax Sinica that the Indian moment truly arrives. The sheer scale and rapidity of China's rise has created space and demand for other propositions and powers, if only to balance the Middle Kingdom's. Indeed, many are now asking what a post-Western world will look like. Can Chairman Xi successfully globalize 'socialism with Chinese characteristics'? While China has certainly enjoyed some measure of success so far, Beijing would be amiss to assess these as irreversible trends. Indeed, China's emerging propositions have themselves made India's, and others', articulations of the world order more attractive. Thought of another way, China's rejection of the liberal international order, and the West's continued evangelism about its utility, have left many countries searching for a median.

India is in a strong position to provide this—an 'India Way'.

For India, the challenge will be to leverage Chinese investments to fuel its growth, even as it offers Asia and the world a democratic model for development and a proposition for security based on international rules and institutions. In other words, the most robust alternative for post-Western world order, barring the China model, may well be the 'India model'. As a result, any Indian response to China's rise must be defined by an overarching Indian grand strategy for leadership in the world order, and it must be engaged with now.

There are two crucial factors that must be kept in mind. The first, of course, is the evolving nature of our societies. The world is transitioning from the third industrial revolution to the fourth, which will be defined by digitization and will elevate the role of human capital and their placements within both highly surveilled and highly open societies. This will present an enormous opportunity for India to become the hub of free and open digital communities. To understand why, consider how China and India were implicated by globalization at the turn of the century.[1] The financial flows from the West to China were primarily in manufacturing industries that relied on low-skill labour. India, meanwhile, emerged as a back end for financial and consumer services. India was part of the industrial chains that required greater trust and human interaction. As we transition into the fourth industrial revolution, elements of transparency and 'similar values' will become even more relevant. Thus, while China may build the physical infrastructure of today, India may well be the most consequential actor for the digital highways that will define globalization in the twenty-first century.

This brings us to our second key factor: India's own trajectory. By the middle of the century, it will rank amongst the three largest economies in the world in real terms. This will coincide with the erstwhile Atlantic community losing its ability to independently sustain and support the international order. India will have to pick up the slack and infect the world order with new energy and purpose. New Delhi's ability to do this will depend on the vision of its role in the world and its ability to foster strategic foresight and build institutional capacity that befits a multitrillion-dollar economy. In this, India must learn from China, which has, with great patience and prescience, built its power and influence in the international order. As India rises, it must similarly learn how to 'act' as a great power. Perhaps the Indian government may have already understood the urgency of this imperative. The most articulate manifestation of this thinking has come from External Affairs Minister S. Jaishankar. In four of his interventions at the Raisina Dialogue and the Observer Research Foundation (ORF), the EAM, who was then foreign secretary, laid out a roadmap for India in these turbulent times with a series of guiding principles.

The first principle relates to India's response to the prevailing 'zeitgeist' of international politics: nationalism as a defining global mood. Around the world, and especially in the transatlantic community, we see a declining appetite for internationalism and multilateral diplomacy. China's rise and the reach of its influence have expanded in tandem with a withdrawal from responsible statecraft by erstwhile powers. India, on the other hand, has mostly been immune to the nationalism bug. Delhi has sought greater voice and responsibility in the international system and it remains an active supporter of global integration based on international rules and institutions. Even as Trump announced the US's withdrawal from the Paris Climate Change Agreement, for example, Prime Minister Modi doubled down on India's commitment and promised to do 'more'. Similarly, at Davos, the he made a case for more globalization and not less. If nationalism is the new normal, said Jaishankar while taking stock of these trends, 'can India make a difference–by being different.'[2] In other words, the foreign secretary argued for more proactive engagement with global governance. Delhi must not only fill the void that traditional guarantors of the international order are leaving behind, but must also articulate a new ethos for multilateralism in a multipolar world.

The second guiding principle relates to the reconfiguration

of global economic governance. At the Raisina Dialogue in 2018, India's then-top diplomat warned that 'non-market economics' threatened to upend economic relations.[3] While he exhibited his customary refrain in describing the challenge, the foreign secretary certainly had China in mind. Complete control over industry by the party-state, and utilization of markets to maximize state power and legitimacy with disregard for corporate independence form the essence of 'capitalism with Chinese characteristics'. The foreign secretary's warning about the 'Beijing Consensus' is also a wake-up call for Indian economic diplomacy, which has mostly been absent from Indian foreign policy. Indeed, geo-economics is making a comeback around the world, with states attempting to capture global markets. The BRI is perhaps the most potent expression of this new normal. India, unfortunately, is often defensive, and not propositional on global economic governance. Saddled with a history of regulation and tariffs, it is hesitant about new trade rules like the RCEP as it is about signing new regulations for the data economy at the G20. However, a leading power cannot play on the back foot. India must learn how trade arrangements, supply chains, economic partnerships and its own domestic regulations can protect and advance its interests in maintaining a rules-based economic order.

Third, India's propositions will be inclusive by design. In other words, India actively seeks and serves multilateralism. The foreign secretary alluded to this during an interaction at the Observer Research Foundation, when he stated that 'issue-based alignments and partnerships' would guide Indian foreign policy priorities.[4] This feature of India's global footprint is defined both by pragmatism and idealism. It is pragmatic because India recognizes that disagreement is likely to be the norm in a multipolar world. Nevertheless, New Delhi is willing and able to lead and participate in coalitions of states on issues of importance and national interest. Consider, for example, India's sustained commitment to tackling climate change, despite the US's intransigence under the Trump administration.

At the same time, the Indian approach, pragmatic as it may be, is also coloured by traditional idealism.[5] India has always preferred to work with partners and institutions. It has rarely exhibited the unilateral streak that defines other large powers. And it has always invested in building platforms of diplomacy and multilateralism, an ethos that will serve the new world order well.

Finally, and most importantly, at the latest edition of the Dialogue in 2019, Jaishankar, who was then briefly with industry following his retirement as foreign secretary, argued that a liberal international order need not be Western-led.[6] Whichever way you dissect the decline of this order today, it is clear that there is a vacuum in leadership and little sense of purpose and direction. There are few countries as suitable to steering the international order at this moment as India. While India may not harbour ambitions of a 'Pax Indica', the 'Idea of India' is likely to have universal appeal. It is an Asian democracy, well integrated into the global economic system, and a non-hegemonic power. Indian propositions for political, economic, and security arrangements are not only likely to be palatable for a large number of states, but also potentially suitable for them, given India's status as an emerging nation. In other words, the ideation and creation of a 'post-Western' liberal order should begin in India.

Taken as a whole, the external affairs minister's pronouncements offer a template for what India's diplomacy as a 'leading power' should seek to achieve. An Indian claim to the stewardship of the liberal world order will not only breathe new life into a struggling system but also offer a response to China's propositions for ordering the world. However, it is not inevitable that India will define the arrangements for a twenty-first-century world order. This will depend on India's willingness to stake this claim. This can happen through its policy postures and an articulation of its state interest, its ability to internalize and stay consistent at home to the values it professes on the global state, and on the appeal of its international leadership to its peers in Asia and around the world. Indeed, this book has devoted much time and effort into documenting China's efforts at remaking the international order in its image and the consequences of these efforts for India. We believe that while this is a necessary catalyst for India's rise, it is only a beginning. In time, India will be capable of bringing together East and West, North and South to put forward a new proposition—one that is as compelling as Pax Sinica. It will offer arrangements for developing states that are inclusive and democratic. Even as Pax Sinica continues to evolve and mature, the coming decades will witness the emergence of the Idea of India. The interaction of these two propositions will invariably define the contours of the world in the twenty-first century.

NOTES

CHAPTER I: A NEW ERA OF STRONGMAN POLITICS

1 Zhenhui Xu, *China 2030: An Analysis of the World Bank's Reform Strategy*, China Research Center, 14 June 2012, https://www.chinacenter.net/2012/china_currents/11-1/china-2030-an-analysis-of-the-world-banks-reform-strategy/

2 David Pilling, 'China's rapid change and missed chances', *Financial Times*, 15 November 2012, https://www.ft.com/content/d7ff0e20-2da2-11e2-9988-00144feabdc0, Accessed 9 July 2019.

3 This section is based on publicly available profiles of Xi Jinping. See, for example, Profile: China's President Xi Jinping, BBC, 25 February 2018, https://www.bbc.com/news/world-asia-pacific-11551399

4 Anant Krishnan, 'The princeling from the grassroots', *The Hindu*, 5 November 2012, https://www.thehindu.com/opinion/op-ed/the-princeling-from-the-grass-roots/article4064948.ece, Accessed on 9 July 2019. (The yellow earth is a reference to the top soil in Shaanxi village, which is a distinctive yellow moss.)

5 Portrait Of Vice President Xi Jinping: 'Ambitious Survivor Of The Cultural Revolution', Public Library of US Diplomacy, WikiLeaks, 16 November 2009, https://wikileaks.org/plusd/cables/09BEIJING3128_a.html, Accessed on 9 July 2019.

6 Profle Xi Jinping: vice president of Peoples Republic of China, *People's Daily*, 16 March 2008, http://en.people.cn/90002/93244/93297/6374355.html

7 Mathias Bolonger, 'Xi Jinping: the compromise candidate', *D.W.*, 30 November 2009, https://www.dw.com/en/xi-jinping-the-compromise-

candidate/a-16331898, Accessed 9 July 2019.

8 Kevin Rudd, 'China's leadership change signals need for new strategic road map with US.', *The Australian*, 19 October 2012, https://www.theaustralian.com.au/national-affairs/opinion/chinas-leadership-change-signals-need-for-new-strategic-road-map-with-us/news-story/5687dddb74079f9066fbfc2e5b6106b9, Accessed 9 July 2019.

9 Jemery Page, Bob Davis and Tom Orlik; 'China's New Boss', *The Wall Street Journal*, 12 November 2012, https://www.wsj.com/articles/SB10001424127887324439804578106860600724862, Accessed 9 July 2019.

10 Nicholas Kristof, 'Looking for a jump start in China', *The New York Times*, 5 January 2013, https://www.nytimes.com/2013/01/06/opinion/sunday/kristof-looking-for-a-jump-start-in-china.html, Accessed 9 July 2019.

11 Joseph Fewsmith, 'Xi Jinping's Fast Start', *China Leadership Monitor* 41, Hoover Institute, https://www.hoover.org/sites/default/files/uploads/documents/CLM41JF.pdf

12 Joanna Chiu, *China's Constitutional Crisis*, 3 September 2013, https://www.theatlantic.com/china/archive/2013/09/chinas-constitutional-crisis/279285/

13 'Chinese Academy of Social Sciences publishes anti-corruption blue book', *Xinhua*, 20 December 2012, http://news.xinhuanet.com/legal/2012-12/20/c_114089170.htm, Accessed 9 July 2019.

14 Simon Denyer, 'As Bo Xilai trial hogs spotlight, arrests show Xi Jinping consolidating control', *Washington Post*, 26 August 2013, https://www.washingtonpost.com/world/as-bo-trial-hogs-spotlight-series-of-arrests-show-xi-consolidating-control/2013/08/26/225f5c16-0e41-11e3-a2b3-5e107edf9897_story.html

15 'China sacks head of state asset regulator Jiang Jiemin amid graft probe', *South China Morning Post*, 2 September 2013, https://www.scmp.com/news/china/article/1302435/china-sacks-head-state-asset-regulator-jiang-jiemin-amid-graft-probe, Accessed 9 July 2019.

16 Pin Hi, Richard McGregor, 'Why is China Purging Its Former Top Security Chief, Zhou Yongkang', *China File*, 17 December 2013, http://www.chinafile.com/conversation/why-china-purging-its-former-top-security-chief-zhou-yongkang

17 *Document 9: A ChinaFile Translation*, 8 November 2013, http://www.chinafile.com/document-9-chinafile-translation, Accessed 9 July 2019.

18 Xi Jinping, *The Governance of China* I, Foreign Language Press, 2017, pp. XX.

19 'Xi says multi-party system didn't work for China', Reuters, 1 April 2014, https://www.reuters.com/article/us-china-politics-xi/xi-says-multi-

party-system-didnt-work-for-china-idUSBREA3107S20140402

20 'America's Pacific Century', Hillary Clinton, Remarks at East-West Centre, Honululu, 10 November 2011, https://2009-2017.state.gov/secretary/20092013clinton/rm/2011/11/176999.htm

21 Remarks by Secretary Panetta at the Shangri-La Dialogue in Singapore, 2 June 2012, https://archive.defence.gov/transcripts/transcript.aspx?transcriptid=5049

22 'Text of Obama's Speech to Parliament', *The Sydney Morning Herald*, 17 November 2011, https://www.smh.com.au/national/text-of-obamas-speech-to-parliament-20111117-1nkcw.html, Accessed 9 July 2019.

23 'Beijing wary of Obama's assertive China policy', Associated Press, 18 November 2011, http://archive.indianexpress.com/news/beijing-wary-of-obama-s-assertive-china-policy/877415/, Accessed 9 July 2019.

24 Henry Kissinger, *On China*, 2nd Edition, New York: Penguin, 2012, p. 546.

25 'Xi urges armed forces loyalty, discipline', *Xinhua*, 11 March 2013, http://www.chinadaily.com.cn/china/2013npc/2013-03/11/content_16299813.htm

26 Graham Allision and Robert Blackwill, 'Interview: Lee Kuan Yew on the Future of US China Relations', *The Atlantic*, 5 March 2013, https://www.theatlantic.com/china/archive/2013/03/interview-lee-kuan-yew-on-the-future-of-us-china-relations/273657/, Accessed 9 July 2019.

27 '"China to pay "great importance" to relations with India": Xi', *Deccan Herald*, 14 January 2013, https://www.deccanherald.com/content/305197/china-pay-importance-relations-india.html, Accessed 9 July 2019.

28 Anant Krishnan, 'What China's Stransition Means for India', *The Hindu*, 3 December 2012, https://www.thehindu.com/opinion/lead/what-chinas-transition-means-for-india/article4156961.ece

29 *India and the World*, Pew Research Center, 10 September 2012, https://www.pewresearch.org/global/2012/09/10/chapter-3-india-and-the-rest-of-the-world/, Accessed 9 July 2019.

30 Gautam Datt, 'US Defence Secretary Leon Panetta identifies India as Linchpin in US game plan to counter China in Asia Pacific', *India Today*, 7 June 2012, https://www.indiatoday.in/india/north/story/leon-panetta-identifies-india-as-linchpin-to-counter-china-104814-2012-06-07, Accessed 9 July 2019.

31 India's GDP per capita stood at $853 in 1990 as compared to China's $839.

32 'Indian Democracy Is Shallow, a Failure', *Hindustan Times*, 28 September

2013, https://www.hindustantimes.com/world/indian-democracy-is-shallow-a-failure/story-gDfmY9QkuYnTqD13Z1mMAK.html, Accessed 9 July 2019.

33 Kevin Rudd, 'Beyond the Pivot', *Foreign Affairs*, March 2013, https://www.foreignaffairs.com/articles/china/2013-02-11/beyond-pivot, Accessed 9 July 2019.

34 Jane Perlze, 'China names its new foreign policy team', *The New York Times*, 16 March 2013, https://www.nytimes.com/2013/03/17/world/asia/china-names-its-new-foreign-policy-team.html, Accessed 9 July 2019.

CHAPTER II: A MULTIPOLAR WORLD WITH CHINESE CHARACTERISTICS

1 'Xi eyes more enabling int'l environment for China's peaceful development', *Xinhua*, 30 November 2014, http://eng.mod.gov.cn/TopNews/2014-11/30/content_4554680.htm

2 Christopher Johnson, 'Thoughts from the Chairman: Xi Jinping Unveils His Foreign Policy Vision', 8 December 2014, https://www.csis.org/analysis/thoughts-chairman-xi-jinping-unveils-his-foreign-policy-vision

3 Wang Yi, 'Exploring the Path of Major Country Diplomacy with Chinese Characteristics,' Remarks at the Second World Peace Forum, 27 June 2013, available online at http://www.fmprc.gov.cn/eng/zxxx/t1053908.shtml, Accessed on 9 July 2019

4 Graham Allison, 'China Doesn't Belong in the BRICS', *The Atlantic*, 26 March, 2013, https://www.theatlantic.com/china/archive/2013/03/china-doesnt-belong-in-the-brics/274363/

5 'BRICS, Emerging Markets and the World Economy: Not Just Straw Men', *The Economist*, 18 June 2009, https://www.economist.com/taxonomy/term/122?page=34, Accessed on 9 July 2019

6 Oliver Stuenkel, *The BRICS and the Future of Global Order*, Lexington Books, New York, 2013. Pp. 14.

7 'The US hegemony ends, the era of global multipolarity enters', *People's Daily*, 24 February 2009, http://en.people.cn/90002/96417/6599374.html, Accessed on 9 July 2019

8 'President Xi urges BRICS, Sino-India Cooperation', *Xinhua*, 20 March 2013, http://www.globaltimes.cn/content/769440.shtml, Accessed on 9 July 2019

9 *Global Trends 2025: A Transformed World*, US National Intelligence Council,

20 November 2008, www.dni.gov/nic/NIC_2025_project.html , Accessed on 9 July 2019

10 'Uganda turns east: Chinese money will build infrastructure says Museven', *Financial Times*, 21 October 2014, https://www.google.com/search?q=Uganda+turns+east%3A+Chinese+money+will+build+infrastructure+says+Museven&oq=Uganda+turns+east%3A+Chinese+money+will+build+infrastructure+says+Museven&aqs=chrome..69i57.227j0j7&sourceid=chrome&ie=UTF-8, Accessed on 9 July 2019

11 'Reinventing Globalization: *China's Second Continent*', Excerpted from Howard French, *China's Second Continent*, USCBC, 24 November 2014, https://www.chinabusinessreview.com/reinventing-globalization-chinas-second-continent/, Accessed on 9 July 2019

12 Lamdo Sanusi, 'Africa must get real about Chinese ties', *Financial Times*, 12 March 2013, https://www.ft.com/content/562692b0-898c-11e2-ad3f-00144feabdc0

13 'Clinton tells developing world to be wary of donors', Reuters, 30 November 2011, https://www.reuters.com/article/us-development-clinton/clinton-tells-developing-world-to-be-wary-of-donors-idUSTRE7AT08J20111130

14 Jim O'Neill; 'A BRICS bank needs a sense of purpose to succeed', 6 August 2013, Livemint, https://www.livemint.com/Opinion/jNWvk7TuWyio1cgVrKyU4N/A-BRICS-bank-needs-a-sense-of-purpose-to-succeed.html, Accessed on 9 July 2019

15 'China Uses Global Crisis to Assert Its Influence,' *Washington Post*, 23 April 2009

16 'Xi Jinping Speaks at the 19th Collective Study Session of the CCP Political Bureau, Stresses Need to Accelerate Free Trade Zone Strategy,' *Xinhua*, 6 December, 2014.

17 'Xi seeks new outlook on foreign affairs', *Xinhua*, 30 November 2014, http://www.china.org.cn/china/2014-11/30/content_34188844_2.htm

18 Robert Zoellick, 'Whither China? From Membership to Responsibility', Remarks to the National Committee on US-China Relations, New York, 21 September 2005, https://www.ncuscr.org/sites/default/files/migration/Zoellick_remarks_notes06_winter_spring.pdf, Accessed on 9 July 2019

19 Jane Perlzez, 'US Opposing China's Answer to World Bank', 9 October 2014, *New York Times*, https://www.nytimes.com/2014/10/10/world/asia/chinas-plan-for-regional-development-bank-runs-into-us-opposition.html, Accessed on 9 July 2019

20 Remarks of Secretary Lew at the World Affairs Council of Seattle on Building a Stronger Global Economy, Department of the Treasury, 12

November 2014, https://www.treasury.gov/press-center/press-releases/Pages/jl2696.aspx

21 'Who Will Pay for Asia's $8 Trillion Infrastructure Gap?', 30 September 2013, https://www.adb.org/news/infographics/who-will-pay-asias-8-trillion-infrastructure-gap

22 'Why China is creating a new "World Bank" for Asia', *The Economist*, 11 November 2014, https://www.economist.com/the-economist-explains/2014/11/11/why-china-is-creating-a-new-world-bank-for-asia

23 Daniel Lim and James Vreeland, 'Regional Organizations and International Politics: Japanese Influence over the Asian Development Bank and the Un Security Council', *World Politics* 65, Issue 1, 2013, pp. 34-72, https://www.cambridge.org/core/journals/world-politics/article/regional-organizations-and-international-politics-japanese-influence-over-the-asian-development-bank-and-the-un-security-council/1AD5B9FD462B1D0CACF4082B8CC26C28, Accessed on 9 July 2019

24 'A despot's guide to foreign aid', *The Economist*, 16 April 2016, https://www.economist.com/middle-east-and-africa/2016/04/16/a-despots-guide-to-foreign-aid, Accessed on 9 July 2019

25 Priyanka Boghani and Erin Smith; 'China will offer Africa aid with "no political strings attached", says Xi', *PRI*, 25 March 2013, https://www.pri.org/stories/2013-03-25/china-will-offer-africa-aid-no-political-strings-attached-says-xi, Accessed on 9 July 2019

26 Evan Feigenbaum; 'China and the World', *Foreign Affairs*, January 2017, https://www.foreignaffairs.com/articles/china/2016-12-12/china-and-world, Accessed on 9 July 2019

27 Howard French, *Everything Under the Heaveans: How the Past Helps China's Push for Global Power*, Knopf; 1st Edition (March 14 2017) , Accessed on 9 July 2019

CHAPTER III: THE WORLD IS 'MODI'FIED

1 *The World in 2050*, PwC, https://www.pwc.com/gx/en/issues/economy/the-world-in-2050.html

2 Ashok Malik, 'The India that Made Modi', European Council on Foreign Relations, November 2015, https://www.ecfr.eu/what_does_india_think/analysis/the_india_that_made_modi, Accessed 9 July 2019

3 C. Raja Mohan, *Modi's World: Expanding India's Sphere of Influence*, HarperCollins, 2015.

4 Brahma Chellany, 'Deconstructing the Modi Foreign Policy', *The Hindu*, 4 December 2014, https://www.thehindu.com/opinion/lead/deconstructing-the-modi-foreign-policy/article6658904.ece

5 BJP, *Election Manifesto 2014* (New Delhi: Bharatiya Janata Party, 2014), 39.

6 Manjari Chatterjee Miller, 'India's Feeble Foreign Policy', *Foreign Affairs*, May/June 2013, https://www.foreignaffairs.com/articles/india/2013-04-03/indias-feeble-foreign-policy, Accessed 9 July 2019

7 'Shri Modi delineates his approach towads governance in first 100 days after coming to power', YouTube, 21 April 2014, https://www.youtube.com/watch?v=mAHq3cfV5Lo, Accessed 9 July, 2019

8 Gideon Rachman, *Easternisation: War and Peace in the Asian Century*, Penguin Random House, 2016, pp. 118

9 'PM Modi outlines dream for India at Madison Square Garden during US visit', *Business Today*, 24 September 2014, https://www.businesstoday.in/current/world/pm-narendra-modi-us-visit-madison-square-garden-nri-visa/story/210860.html, Accessed 9 July 2019

10 'Text of 37th Singapore Lecture, "India's Singapore Story", by Prime Minister during his visit to Singapore', Press Information Bureau, 23 November 2015, http://pib.gov.in/newsite/PrintRelease.aspx?relid=131821

11 Ibid.

12 'Text of Address by PM at Nazarbayev University, Astana, Kazakhstan', Press Information Bureau, 7 July 2015

13 Ted Piccone, *Five Rising Democracies and the Fate of the International Liberal Order*, Brookings Institution Press, 23 February 2016

14 Henry Kissinger, *Diplomacy*, Simon & Schuster, 1994.

15 'Full text of Narendra Modi's interview', *Business Standard*, 28 May 2015, http//:www.business-standard.com/ article/economy-policy/full-text-of-pm-narendra-modi-s-interview-to-pti-115052800367_1.html.

16 Jaishankar lauds Modi's proactive foreign policy, Tharoor slams "yo-yo" on Pakistan', *Business Standard*, 17 July 2015, https://www.business-standard.com/article/news-ians/jaishankar-lauds-modi-s-proactive-foreign-policy-tharoor-slams-yo-yo-on-pakistan-115071701391_1.html

17 'IISS Fullerton Lecture by Dr. S. Jaishankar, Foreign Secretary in Singapore', Speech presented at the International Institute for Strategic Studies, Singapore, 20 July 2015, Accessed 9 July 2019

18 Ian Hall, 'Narendra Modi and India's normative power', *International Affairs* 93, Issue No. 1, 2017, https://www.chathamhouse.org/publication/ia/narendra-modi-and-india-s-normative-power, Accessed 9 July 2019

19 C. Raja Mohan, *Modi's World: Expanding India's Sphere of Influence,* HarperCollins, 2015.

20 'India, China foreign ministers hold 'frank, substantive' talks', Press Trust of India, 8 June 2014, https://economictimes.indiatimes.com/news/politics-and-nation/india-china-foreign-ministers-hold-frank-substantive-talks/articleshow/36256346.cms?from=mdr

21 Howard French, 'China's Dangerous Game', *The Atlantic*, November 2014, https://www.theatlantic.com/magazine/archive/2014/11/chinas-dangerous-game/380789/

22 Sanjeev Miglani, 'Indian leader heading to Bangladesh with China on his mind', Reuters, 28 May 2015, https://www.reuters.com/article/india-bangladesh-china/indian-leader-heading-to-bangladesh-with-china-on-his-mind-idUSL3N0YG2QG20150527, Accessed 9 July 2019

23 Quoted from Gideon Rachman, *Easternization: War and Peace in the Asian Century*, Bodley Head, 2016, pp. 126

24 Mitsuru Obe and Niharika Mandhana, 'India and Japan Pursue Closer Ties to Counter China', *Wall Street Journal*, 1 September 2014, https://www.wsj.com/articles/indias-prime-minister-narendra-modi-wants-closer-ties-with-japan-to-counter-china-1409555754

25 Rory Medcalf and Linda Jakobson, 'The Perception Gap: Reading China's Maritime Objectives in the Indo-Pacific Asia', Lowy Institute, 23 June 2015, https://www.lowyinstitute.org/publications/perception-gap-reading-chinas-maritime-objectives-indo-pacific-asia, Accessed 9 July 2019

26 Xi Jinping, 'Towards and Asian Century of Prosperity', *The Hindu*, September 17 2014, https://www.thehindu.com/opinion/op-ed/towards-an-asian-century-of-prosperity/article6416553.ece

27 Liu Zongyi; 'Modi ready to do business with China'. *Global Times*, 19 May, 2015, http://www.globaltimes.cn/content/861112.shtml, Accessed 9 July 2019

28 Press Statement by Prime Minister during the visit of President Xi Jinping of China to India (18 September 2014), https://www.mea.gov.in/Speeches-Statements.htm?dtl/24014/

29 Sanjeev Miglani, 'With canal and hut, India stands up to China on disputed frontier', Reuters, 25 September 2014, https://www.reuters.com/article/india-china-modi-chumar-army-ladakh/insight-with-canal-and-hut-india-stands-up-to-china-on-disputed-frontier-idINKCN0HJ2FU20140924, Accessed 9 July 2019

30 India Poll 2013, Lowy Institute, 20 May 2013, https://www.lowyinstitute.org/publications/india-poll-2013

31 'Xi Jinping asks Chinese Army to be ready for regional war', *India Today*, 23 September 2014, https://www.indiatoday.in/world/story/xi-jinping-chinese-army-pla-regional-war-293871-2014-09-22

32 Peter Baker and Gardiner Harris, 'US and India Share Sense of Unease Over China', *The New York Times*, 26 January 2015, https://www.nytimes.com/2015/01/27/world/us-and-india-share-sense-of-unease-over-china.html, Accessed 9 July 2019

33 'Mapping the Global Future', National Intelligence Council, December 2004, https://www.dni.gov/files/documents/Global%20Trends_Mapping%20the%20Global%20Future%202020%20Project.pdf, Accessed 9 July 2019

CHAPTER IV: BELT AND ROAD INITIATIVE: A COMMUNITY OF COMMON DESTINY

1 'President Xi Proposes Silk Road Economic Belt', *China Daily*, 7 September 2013, http://www.chinadaily.com.cn/china/2013xivisitcenterasia/2013-09/07/content_16951811.htm, Accessed on 9 July 2019

2 'President Xi gives speech to Indonesia's parliament', *China Daily*, 2 November 2013, http://www.chinadaily.com.cn/china/2013xiapec/2013-10/02/content_ 17007915.htm

3 *Meeting Asia's Infrastructure Needs*, Asian Development Bank, February 2017, https://www.adb.org/publications/asia-infrastructure-needs, Accessed on 9 July 2019

4 Therasa Fallon, 'The New Silk Road: Xi Jinping's Grand Strategy for Eurasia', *American Foreign Policy Interest: The Journal of the National Committee on American Foreign Policy*, 37:3, 2015 140-147, DOI: 10.1080/10803920.2015.1056682, Accessed on 9 July 2019

5 The project was renamed from 'One Belt One Road' to 'Belt and Road Initiative' in 2015, because Chinese officials worried that pejorative use of the word 'one' would lead to the perception that only China would build these infrastructure networks.

6 Richard Harris, 'China and the World', *International Affairs* 35, Issue No.2, 1959, pp. 161-169, https://www.jstor.org/stable/2605294?seq=1#page_scan_tab_contents, Accessed on 9 July 2019

7 Phillip Hoffman, 'How Europe Conquered the World', *Foreign Affairs*, 7 October 2015, https://www.foreignaffairs.com/articles/europe/2015-10-07/how-europe-conquered-world

8 *Global Trends 2030 Report*, National Intelligence Council, 2012, https://

www.atlanticcouncil.org/publications/reports/global-trends-2030-alternative-worlds, Accessed on 9 July 2019

9 Graham Allison and Robert Blackwill, 'Interview: Lee Kuan Yew on the Future of US-China Relations', *The Atlantic*, 5 March 2013, https://www.theatlantic.com/china/archive/2013/03/interview-lee-kuan-yew-on-the-future-of-us-china-relations/273657/, Accessed on 9 July 2019

10 'At the 27th Collective Study Session of the CCP Political Bureau; Xi Jinping Stresses the Need to Push Forward the System of Global Governance', *Xinhua*, 13 October 2015

11 'Chinese investment in Europe: record flows and growing imbalances', Mercator Institute for Chinese Studies, 3 January 2017, https://www.merics.org/en/papers-on-china/chinese-investment-europe-record-flows-and-growing-imbalances

12 John Seaman, Mikki Huatari and Miguel Iglesias, 'Chinese Investment in Europe', European Think Tank Network on China, December 2017, https://www.ifri.org/sites/default/files/atoms/files/etnc_reports_2017_final_20dec2017.pdf

13 Robin Emmott and Angeliki Koutantou, 'Greece blocks EU statement on China human rights at UN', Reuters, June 18, 2017, https://www.reuters.com/article/us-eu-un-rights/greece-blocks-eu-statement-on-china-human-rights-at-u-n-idUSKBN1990FP

14 'EU's statement on South China Sea reflects divisions,' Reuters, 15 July 2016, https://www.reuters.com/article/southchinasea-ruling-eu-idUSL8N1A130Y

15 Kevin Rudd, 'The West isn't ready for the rise of China', *New Statesmen*, 11 July 2012, https://www.newstatesman.com/politics/international-politics/2012/07/kevin-rudd-west-isnt-ready-rise-china, Accessed on 9 July 2019

16 Ye Zicheng, *Inside China's Grand Strategy: The Perspective from the Peoples Republic*, The University Press of Kentucky, 2011.

17 Robert Giplin, *War and Change in World Politics*, Cambridge University Press; 25 November 1983, pp. 9.

18 'The Central Conference on Work Relating to Foreign Affairs was Held in Beijing', Ministry of Foreign Affairs of the Peoples Republic of China, 29 November 2014, https://www.fmprc.gov.cn/mfa_eng/zxxx_662805/t1215680.shtml, Accessed on 9 July 2019

19 Party Committee Central Group of the Ministry of Foreign Affairs, 'The New Realm of Diplomatic Theory of Socialism with Chinese Characteristics', *Seeking Truth*, 16 February 2013, pp. 4.

20 John Ikenberry, 'The Rise of China and the Future of the West',

Foreign Affairs, January 2008, https://archive.nytimes.com/www.nytimes.com/cfr/world/20080101faessay_v87n1_ikenberry.html?_r=1&pagewanted=all, Accessed on 9 July 2019

21 Henry Kissinger, *World Order*, New York: Penguin Books, 2015, p. 230.

22 Annual Report 2016, US Congressional Executive Commission on China, 6 October 2016, https://www.govinfo.gov/content/pkg/CHRG-114hhrg21471/html/CHRG-114hhrg21471.htm, Accessed on 9 July 2019

23 Jason Dean, Andrew Browne and Shai Oster, 'China's "State Capitalism" Sparks a Global Backlash', *Wall Street Journal*, 16 November 2010, https://www.wsj.com/articles/SB100014240527487035149045756027310063151 98, Accessed on 9 July 2019

24 Keith Bradsher, 'Amid Tensions, China Blocks Vital Exports to Japan', *The New York Times*, 22 September 2010, https://www.nytimes.com/2010/09/23/business/global/23rare.html

25 'Baseline Study on the Human Rights Impacts and Implications of Mega-Infrastructure Investment', The Office of the UN High Commissioner for Human Rights, 6 July 2017, https://www.ohchr.org/Documents/Issues/Development/DFI/MappingStudyontheHRRiskImplications_MegaInfrastructureInvestment.pdf, Accessed on 9 July 2019

26 Jonathan Hillman, 'China's Belt and Road Initiative: Five Years Later', *CSIS*, 25 January 2018, https://www.csis.org/analysis/chinas-belt-and-road-initiative-five-years-later-0, Accessed on 9 July 2019

27 Atul Aneja, 'China rejects Hague tribunal ruling as "null and void"', *The Hindu*,12 July 2016, https://www.thehindu.com/news/international/China-rejects-Hague-tribunal-ruling-as-%E2%80%9Cnull-and-void%E2%80%9D/article14486651.ece

28 Liue Mingfu, *The China Dream*, CN Time Books Inc., 30 June 2015.

29 'China's Policies on Asia-Pacific Security Cooperation', The State Council Information Office of the PRC, 11 January 2017, http://english.gov.cn/archive/white_paper/2017/01/11/content_281475539078636.htm, Accessed on 9 July 2019

30 John J. Mearsheimer, 'The Gathering Storm: China's Challenge to US Power in Asia', *The Chinese Journal of International Politics*, Volume 3, Issue 4, Winter 2010, Pages 381–396, https://doi.org/10.1093/cjip/poq016, Accessed on 9 July 2019

31 Evan Feigenbaum, 'Reluctant Stakeholder: Why China's Highly Strategic Brand of Revisionism is More Challenging Than Washington Thinks', *Macro Polo*, 27 April 2018, https://macropolo.org/analysis/reluctant-stakeholder-why-chinas-highly-strategic-brand-of-revisionism-is-more-challenging-than-washington-thinks/, Accessed on 10 July 2019.

32 Kevin Rudd, Alastair Buchan Memorial Lecture, 16 December 2013, http://kevinrudd.com/2013/12/16/alastair-buchan-memorial-lecture/
33 Chris Buckley, 'China's Communist Party Declared Xi Jinping 'Core Leader'', *The New York Times*, 27 October 2016, https://www.nytimes.com/2016/10/28/world/asia/xi-jinping-china.html

CHAPTER V: CONTESTED NARRATIVES

1 *Global Tends 2030: Alternate Worlds*, US National Intelligence Council, December 2012, https://www.dni.gov/files/documents/GlobalTrends_2030.pdf, pp.15 , Accessed on 9 July 2019
2 'The rise of the trillion-dollar state economies', LiveMint, 2 March 2018, https://www.livemint.com/Opinion/a1gYUgQSCEExIRkC2TDxpK/The-rise-of-the-trilliondollar-state-economies.html
3 Xi Jinping; 'Towards an Asian Century of Prosperity', *The Hindu*, 20 April 2014, https://www.thehindu.com/opinion/op-ed/towards-an-asian-century-of-prosperity/article6416553.ece, Accessed on 9 July 2019
4 'Building ties for the 21st century', *The Hindu*, 1 April 2015.
5 'India expresses concern over China-Pakistan Economic Corridor', Press Trust of India, 14 April 2014, https://economictimes.indiatimes.com/news/politics-and-nation/india-expresses-concern-over-china-pakistan-economic-corridor/articleshow/33752151.cms?from=mdr
6 Shiv Shankar Menon, Speech, 'The Political Prospects, Effects and Intent of BRI', *Bharatshakti*, 24 April 2017, https://bharatshakti.in/the-political-prospects-effects-and-intent-of-bri/, Accessed on 9 July 2019
7 Transcript of Media Briefing on Prime Minister's forthcoming visits to China, Mongolia and Republic of Korea, MEA, 12 May 2015, https://www.mea.gov.in/outoging-visit-detail.htm?25228/Transcript+of+Media+Briefing+on+Prime+Ministers+forthcoming+visits+to+China+Mongolia+and+Republic+of+Korea+May+12+2015, Accessed on 9 July 2019
8 'India, Pakistan spar over economic corridor passing through PoK', *Hindustan Times*, 1 June 2015, https://www.hindustantimes.com/india/india-pakistan-spar-over-economic-corridor-passing-through-pok/story-GKbLUopoolvckfiGQbjllM.html
9 Charu Kastur, 'India wrinkle on China silk', *The Telegraph*, 21 July 2015, https://www.telegraphindia.com/india/india-wrinkle-on-china-silk/cid/1479577, Accessed on 19 July 2019
10 'Sri Lanka opens $292 million Chinese-funded airport highway', Reuters, 27 October 2013, https://www.reuters.com/article/us-srilanka-china-

highway/sri-lanka-opens-292-million-chinese-funded-airport-highway-idUSBRE99Q06G20131027

11 Atif Ansar and Bent Flyvbjerg, 'Too Much of a Good Thing China's Infrastructure Boom Threatens Its Economic Prosperity', *Reconnecting Asia*, CSIS, 7 December 2016, https://reconnectingasia.csis.org/analysis/entries/too-much-good-thing/, Accessed on 9 July 2019

12 Devin Thorne and Ben Spavak, *Harboured Ambitions*, C4ADS, 2018, https://c4ads.org/reports, pp.24

13 Shyam Saran, 'What China's One Belt and One Road Strategy Means for India, Asia and the World', *The Wire*, 9 October 2015, https://thewire.in/external-affairs/what-chinas-one-belt-and-one-road-strategy-means-for-india-asia-and-the-world

14 Speech by foreign secretary at Raisina Dialogue in New Delhi, 2 March 2016, https://mea.gov.in/Speeches-Statements.htm?dtl/26433/Speech_by_Foreign_Secretary_at_Raisina_Dialogue_in_New_Delhi_2 March_2015

15 Melissa Chan, 'Philippine President Rodrigo Duterte Tells Obama to "Go to Hell"', *Time*, 4 October 2016, https://time.com/4517741/philippine-president-obama-hell/, Accessed on 9 July 2019

16 Max Boot, 'Duterte's Flip-Flop Into Bed With China Is a Disaster for the United States', *Foreign Policy*, 20 October 2016, https://foreignpolicy.com/2016/10/20/rodrigo-dutertes-flip-flop-into-bed-with-china-is-a-disaster-for-the-united-states-south-china-sea/

17 Joseph Sipalan, 'Malaysia's Najib risks backlash at home after deals with China', Reuters, 7 November 2016, https://www.reuters.com/article/us-malaysia-china/malaysias-najib-risks-backlash-at-home-after-deals-with-china-idUSKBN1320EY

18 'Scholars and Media on China's Cultural Soft Power', Wilson Centre, https://www.wilsoncenter.org/scholars-and-media-chinas-cultural-soft-power, Accessed on 9 July 2019

19 Jeff Smith, 'China and Sri Lanka: Between a Dream and a Nightmare', *The Diplomat*, 18 November 2016, https://thediplomat.com/2016/11/china-and-sri-lanka-between-a-dream-and-a-nightmare/

20 'Not many nations get a second chance at democracy': Mohamed Nasheed, ORF, 9 July 2019, https://www.orfonline.org/expert-speak/not-many-nations-get-second-chance-democracy-mohamed-nasheed-52882/

21 Dirk van der Kley, 'Can Central Asia's Poorest States Pay Back Their Debts to China', *The Diplomat*, 1 December 2017, https://thediplomat.com/2017/12/can-central-asias-poorest-states-pay-back-their-debts-to-china/

22 'Kyrgyzstan PM Sariyev resigns after cabinet accused of graft', Reuters, 11 April 2016, https://www.reuters.com/article/us-kyrgyzstan-primeminister-resignation/kyrgyzstan-pm-sariyev-resigns-after-cabinet-accused-of-graft-idUSKCN0X80WM

23 'Kolkata: Lone Indian link in China's Mega Maritime Silk Road', Press Trust of India, 28 March 2015, https://economictimes.indiatimes.com/news/politics-and-nation/kolkata-lone-indian-link-in-chinas-mega-maritime-silk-road/articleshow/46729153.cms

24 'Merkel: Germany backs Belt and Road Initiative, wishes China's forum success', *Xinhua*, 26 April 2017, http://www.xinhuanet.com//english/2017-04/26/c_136237243.htm

25 Sutirtho Patranobis, 'UN support for China project passing through PoK puts India's claim in jeopardy', *Hindustan Times*, 18 March 2017, https://www.hindustantimes.com/world-news/un-security-council-resolution-includes-china-s-bri-india-s-pok-claims-in-jeopardy/story-k6isroFAMdnlA6NtX4nPKN.html

26 Devirupa Mitra, 'China Quietly Deletes Ambassador's Offer to "Rename CPEC" from Embassy Website', *The Wire*, 9 May 2017, https://thewire.in/diplomacy/cpec-obor-china-india-rename

27 'Official Spokesperson's response to a query on participation of India in OBOR/BRI Forum', MEA, 13 May 2017, https://mea.gov.in/media-briefings.htm?dtl/28463/Official+Spokespersons+response+to+a+query+on+participation+of+India+in+OBORBRI+Forum, Accessed on 9 July 2019

28 'China's Xi hails Belt and Road as "project of the century"', *Financial Times*, 14 May 2017, https://www.ft.com/content/88d584a2-385e-11e7-821a-6027b8a20f23

29 'India-Bhutan Friendship Treaty', 8 August 1949, https://www.refworld.org/docid/3ae6b4d620.html

30 'Recent Developments in Doklam Area', MEA, 30 June 2017, https://www.mea.gov.in/press-releases.htm?dtl/28572/Recent_Developments_in_Doklam_Area, Accessed on 9 July 2019

31 'Foreign Ministry Spokesperson Geng Shuang's Remarks on Indian Border Troops Overstepping China-India Boundary at Sikkim Section', Ministry of Foreign Affairs, Peoples Republic of China, 26 June 2017, http://ye.china-embassy.org/eng/fyrth/t1473280.htm, Accessed on 9 July 2019

32 'No Scope for "Compromise," Withdraw Your Troops, China Tells India As Sikkim Stand-Off Continues', *The Wire*, 4 July 2017, https://thewire.in/diplomacy/pti-special-china-says-dokalam-situation-grave-rules, Accessed on 9 July 2019

33 Oriana Skylar Mastro and Arzan Tarapore; 'Countering Chinese Coercion: The Case of Doklam,' War on the Rocks, 29 August 2017, https://warontherocks.com/2017/08/countering-chinese-coercion-the-case-of-doklam/, Accessed on 9 July 2019

34 K.J.M. Varma, 'Chinese Army conducts live-fire drills in Tibet plateau amid Sikkim standoff,' Livemint, 17 July 2017, https://www.livemint.com/Politics/ycfwMXJ1NShJ1SQPleX6lO/Chinese-Army-conducts-live-fire-drills-in-Tibet.html

35 Ananth Krishnan, 'Withdraw, capture or get killed: Ex-Chinese diplomat's 3 options on Doklam', *India Today*, 20 July 2017, https://www.indiatoday.in/india/story/doklam-war-attack-chinese-diplomat-gives-india-options-1025281-2017-07-20, Accessed on 9 July 2019

36 'What if we enter Kalapani, Kashmir: China to India', *The Economic Times*, 12 July 2018, https://economictimes.indiatimes.com/news/defence/what-if-we-enter-kalapani-kashmirchina-to-india/articleshow/59972866.cms?from=mdr, Accessed on 9 July 2019

37 'India will suffer worse losses than 1962 if it incites border clash', *Global Times*, 4 July 2017, http://www.globaltimes.cn/content/1054925.shtml, Accessed on 9 July 2019

38 John Glover, 'This standoff is China telling India to accept changing realities', *South China Morning Post*, 16 July 2017, https://www.scmp.com/week-asia/geopolitics/article/2102547/standoff-china-telling-india-accept-changing-realities, Accessed on 9 July 2019

39 'Spotlight: What's behind India's illegal trespassing into China?', *Xinhua*, 19 August 2017, http://www.xinhuanet.com//english/2017-08/19/c_136539497.htm, Accessed on 9 July 2019

40 Yuji Kuronuma, 'China woos Bhutan with $10 billion in standoff with India', *Nikkei Asia Review*, 26 August 2017, http://southasiajournal.net/china-woos-bhutan-with-10-billion-in-standoff-with-india/

41 Yimou Lee and Wa Lone, 'China's $10 billion strategic project in Myanmar sparks local ire', Reuters, 9 June 2017, https://www.reuters.com/article/us-china-silkroad-myanmar-sez/chinas-10-billion-strategic-project-in-myanmar-sparks-local ire-idUSKBN18Z327

42 Dipanjan Roy Chaudhury, 'Chinese loans may put Bangladesh in debt trap', *The Economic Times*, 17 June 2017, https://economictimes.indiatimes.com/news/politics-and-nation/chinese-loans-may-put-bangladesh-in-debt-trap/articleshow/59185012.cms?from=mdr

43 Dipanjan Roy Chaudury, 'Chinese company bags Maldivian Island on 50-year lease', *The Economic Times*, 30 December 2016, https://economictimes.indiatimes.com/news/politics-and-

nation / chinese-companies-bags-maldivian-island-on-50-year-lease / articleshow / 56245729.cms

44 Counter-Coercion Series, Scarborough Shoal Standoff, Asia Maritime Transparency Initiative, CSIS, https: / / amti.csis.org / counter-co-scarborough-standoff /

45 Ajai Shukla, 'Doklam faceoff: Motives, stakes and what lies ahead?', *Business Standard*, 19 July 2017, http: / / ajaishukla.blogspot.com / 2017 / 07 / doklam-faceoff-motives-stakes-and-what.html, Accessed on 9 July 2019

46 Dipanjan Roy Chaudury, 'Diplomatic channels engaged in defusing Doklam standoff: S Jaishankar', *The Economic Times*, 19 July 2017, https: / / economictimes.indiatimes.com / news / politics-and-nation / diplomatic-channels-engaged-in-defusing-doklam-standoff-s-jaishankar / articleshow / 59656801.cms

47 'US supports "return of status quo" on Doklam issue: Official', *The Economic Times*, 18 August 2017, https: / / economictimes.indiatimes. com / news / defence / us-supports-return-of-status-quo-on-doklam-issue-official / articleshow / 60241209.cms?from=mdr

48 Abhijnan Rej, 'India's clever use of the BRICS card in Doklam standoff', Livemint, 31 August 2017, https: / / www.livemint.com / Opinion / c4ws2jwOqP7ALa7Y0RbC1M / Indias-clever-use-of-the-BRICS-card-in-Doklam-standoff-reso.html

49 'China claims India has withdrawn troops in Doklam, silent on plans to build road', *Economic Times*, 1 September 2017, https: / / economictimes. indiatimes.com / news / defence / china-claims-india-has-withdrawn-troops-in-doklam-silent-on-plans-to-build-road / articleshow / 60261118. cms?from=mdr, Accessed on 9 July 2019

50 Taylor Fravel, 'Why India Did Not "Win" The Standoff With China', *War on the Rocks*, 1 September 2017, https: / / warontherocks.com / 2017 / 09 / why-india-did-not-win-the-standoff-with-china / , Accessed on 9 July 2019

CHAPTER VI: INDIA'S SPACE TO MANOEUVRE

1 'Maldives election: Opposition defeats China-backed Abdulla Yameen', BBC, 24 September 2018, https: / / www.bbc.com / news / world-asia-45623126

2 'President launches US$400m airport runway project', *Maldives Independent*, 27 February 2017, https: / / maldivesindependent.com / business / president-launches-us400m-airport-runway-project-129040

3 Robert Manning and Bharath Gopalaswamy, 'Is Abdulla Yameen Handing

Over the Maldives to China?', *Foreign Policy*, 21 March 2018, https://foreignpolicy.com/2018/03/21/is-abdulla-yameen-handing-over-the-maldives-to-china/

4 David Brewster, 'Beyond the String of Pearls: is there really a Sino-Indian security dilemma in the Indian Ocean?', *Journal of the Indian Ocean Region*, Vol. 10, No. 2, 2014.

5 'Present Dimensions of the Indian Foreign Policy', Address by foreign secretary Mr Shyam Saran at Shanghai Institute of International Studies, Shanghai, 11 January 2006, https://www.mea.gov.in/Speeches-Statements.htm?dtl/2078/Present+Dimensions+of+the+Indian+Foreign+Policy++Address+by+Foreign+Secretary+Mr+Shyam+Saran+at+Shanghai+Institute+of+International+Studies+Shanghai, Accessed on 9 July 2019

6 'South Asia's $2.5 Trillion Infrastructure Gap', World Bank, 2 April 2014, https://www.worldbank.org/en/news/feature/2014/04/02/south-asia-trillion-infrastructure-gap

7 'Chinese Investments in India's Neighbourhood', *Gateway House*, 12 March 2018, https://www.gatewayhouse.in/chinese-investments-in-indias-neighbourhood/

8 Gopal Sharma, 'Nepal restores $2.5 billion hydropower plant contract to Chinese firm', Reuters, 23 September 2018, https://www.reuters.com/article/us-china-nepal-hydropower/nepal-restores-2-5-billion-hydropower-plant-contract-to-chinese-firm-idUSKCN1M30CZ

9 'Second Nepal-China joint military drill in September: Report', *The Hindu*, 21 July 2018, https://www.thehindu.com/news/international/second-nepal-china-joint-military-drill-in-september-report/article24482667.ece

10 'China's huge Rakhine investment behind its tacit backing of Myanmar on Rohingyas', *The Times of India*, 26 September 2017, https://timesofindia.indiatimes.com/world/china/china-will-back-myanmar-on-rohingya-crisis-because-it-is-investing-in-rakhine/articleshow/60845089.cms

11 Simon Denyer, 'The Push and Pull of China's Orbit', *The Washington Post*, September 2015, https://www.washingtonpost.com/sf/world/2015/09/05/the-push-and-pull-of-chinas-orbit/

12 Asit Ranjan Mishra and Elizabeth Roche, 'India extends $4.5 billion loan to Bangladesh', Livemint, 5 October 2017, https://www.livemint.com/Politics/PJNGy9mN1sOLFqVTKKdI5L/Bangladesh-signs-45-billion-loan-deal-with-India.html

13 Raga Sirilal, 'India to invest $2 billion in Sri Lanka in next four years: Nirmala Sitharaman', Livemint, 27 September 2016, https://www.livemint.com/Politics/S3FsOM71PTgS7OS6WExKpK/India-to-invest-2-

billion-in-Sri-Lanka-in-next-four-years.html

14 David Barboza, Marc Santora and Alexandra Stevenson, 'China Seeks Influence in Europe, One Business Deal at a Time', *The New York Times*, 12 August 2018, https://www.nytimes.com/2018/08/12/business/china-influence-europe-czech-republic.html, Accessed on 9 July 2019

15 Abdoulaye Wade; 'Time for the west to practice what it preaches', *Financial Times*, 23 January 2008, https://www.ft.com/content/5d347f88-c897-11dc-94a6-0000779fd2ac, Accessed on 9 July 2019

16 'Xi urges breaking new ground in major country diplomacy with Chinese characteristics', *Xinhua*, 24 June 2018, http://www.xinhuanet.com/english/2018-06/24/c_137276269.htm, Accessed on 9 July 2019

17 Steven Feldstein, 'China Is Exporting AI Surveillance Technology to Countries around the World', *Newsweek*, 24 April 2019, https://www.newsweek.com/china-ai-surveillance-technology-world-1403762

18 Go Yamada, 'Is China's Belt and Road working? A progress report from eight countries', *Nikkei Asian Review*, 28 March 2018, https://asia.nikkei.com/Spotlight/Cover-Story/Is-China-s-Belt-and-Road-working-A-progress-report-from-eight-countries, Accessed on 9 July 2019

19 'Malaysia to renegotiate ECRL terms- Dr Mahathir', Reuters, 27 May 2018, https://www.nst.com.my/news/nation/2018/05/373682/malaysia-renegotiate-ecrl-terms-dr-m, Accessed on 9 July 2019

20 'Rajapaksa threatens to overturn deal with China on Hambantota port', *The New Indian Express*, 16 December 2016, http://www.newindianexpress.com/world/2016/dec/16/rajapaksa-threatens-to-overturn-deal-with-china-on-hambantota-port-1549831--1.html

21 Pranab Dhal Samanta, 'Blow to Beijing: Bangladesh blacklists Chinese infrastructure firm', *The Print*, 18 January 2018, https://theprint.in/india/governance/blow-beijing-bangladesh-blacklists-chinese-infrastructure-firm/30289/

22 Yuichi Nitta, 'Myanmar cuts cost of China-funded port project by 80%', *Nikkei Asia Review*, 18 September 2018, https://asia.nikkei.com/Spotlight/Belt-and-Road/Myanmar-cuts-cost-of-China-funded-port-project-by-80

23 'IMF bailout package to Pakistan to pay off Chinese debts? US raises concern', Press Trust of India, 19 June 2019, https://www.business-standard.com/article/pti-stories/us-pushes-for-conditionality-in-imf-bailout-package-to-pakistan-119061900196_1.html

24 Prashant Jha, 'How India is dealing with China: Improve ties but stay alert', *Hindustan Times*, 12 July 2018, https://www.hindustantimes.com/india-news/how-india-is-dealing-with-china-improve-ties-but-stay-alert/story-ej6Dy9PArfncR5qhoxj4PI.html, Accessed on 9 July 2019

25 Prime Minister's Keynote Address at Shangri La Dialogue, Ministry of External Affairs, 1 June 2018, https://www.mea.gov.in/Speeches-Statements.htm?dtl/29943/Prime+Ministers+Keynote+Address+at+Shangri+La+Dialogue+June+01+2018, Accessed on 9 July 2019

26 'US backs India's opposition to China's One Belt, One Road initiative', *Hindustan Times*, 4 October 2017, https://www.hindustantimes.com/world-news/us-backs-india-s-opposition-to-china-s-one-belt-one-road-initiative/story-mgOIpaVs3i65gtaNRxzMNI.html, Accessed on 9 July 2019

27 'Defining Our Relationship with India for the Next Century: An Address by US Secretary of State Rex Tillerson', CSIS, 18 October 2017, https://www.csis.org/events/defining-our-relationship-india-next-century-address-us-secretary-state-rex-tillerson/

28 'Shared Vision of India-Indonesia Maritime Cooperation in the Indo-Pacific', MEA, 30 May 2018, https://mea.gov.in/bilateral-documents.htm?dtl/29933/Shared_Vision_of_IndiaIndonesia_Maritime_Cooperation_in_the_IndoPacific

CHAPTER VII: BEYOND THE BELT AND ROAD—PATHWAYS TO GLOBAL POWER

1 James McAuley and Gerry Shih, 'The Chinese head of Interpol has disappeared—in China', *The Washington Post*, 5 October 2018, https://www.washingtonpost.com/world/europe/the-chinese-head-of-interpol-has-disappeared--in-china/2018/10/05/4e4878c2-c88f-11e8-9c0f-2ffaf6d422aa_story.html

2 Yang Jiechi, 'Promoting the Building of a Community of Human Destiny', *Peoples Daily*, 19 November 2017, http://opinion.people.com.cn/n1/2017/1119/c1003-29654654.html, Accessed on 9 July 2019

3 Shiping Tang, 'China and the Future International Order', *Rising Powers and the International Order* 32, Issue 1, 2018, pp.31-43, https://www.cambridge.org/core/journals/ethics-and-international-affairs/article/china-and-the-future-international-orders/3E7B1539238F30E8A243164C830E7162, Accessed on 9 July 2019

4 'The Central Conference on Work Relating to Foreign Affairs was Held in Beijing', Ministry of Foreign Affairs of the Peoples Republic of China, 29 November 2014, https://www.fmprc.gov.cn/mfa_eng/zxxx_662805/t1215680.shtml, Accessed on 9 July 2019

5 'Xi calls for Reforms on Global Governance', *Xinhua*, 29 September 2016,

http://www.chinadaily.com.cn/china/2016-09/29/content_26931697.htm, Accessed on 9 July 2019

6 Kevin Rudd on Xi Jinping, 'China and the Global Order', Speech at the Lee Kuan Yew School of Public Policy, National University of Singapore, 26 June 2018, https://asiasociety.org/policy-institute/kevin-rudd-xi-jinping-china-and-global-order, Accessed on 9 July 2019

7 'Chinese President Xi Jinping's 2016 New Year Message', Ministry of Foreign Affairs of the People's Republic of China, 31 December 2015, available at http://www.fmprc.gov.cn/mfa_eng/wjdt_665385/zyjh_665391/t1331985.shtml

8 'Liu Fang re-elected ICAO secretary general', *Xinhua*, 17 March 2018, http://www.xinhuanet.com/english/2018-03/17/c_137044111.htm

9 'Asia Pacific Leads 20-Year Passenger Demand Forecast', IATA, https://www.iata.org/about/worldwide/asia_pacific/Pages/Asia-Pacific-20-Year-Forecast.aspx

10 'World Bank Group gives "number two" job to Chinese Official Yang Shaolin', SCMP, 13 January 2016, https://www.scmp.com/news/china/diplomacy-defence/article/1900491/world-bank-group-gives-number-two-job-chinese-official

11 Charlotte Gao, 'A Community of Shared Future: One Short Phrase for UN, One Big Victory for China?', *The Diplomat*, 5 November 2017, https://thediplomat.com/2017/11/a-community-of-shared-future-one-short-phrase-for-un-one-big-victory-for-china/, Accessed on 9 July 2019

12 '"Shared future" vision provides answers', *China Daily*, 13 April 2018, http://en.people.cn/n3/2018/0413/c90000-9448845.html, Accessed on 9 July 2019

13 John Fisher, 'China's "Win-Win" Resolution Is Anything But', Human Rights Watch, 5 March 2018, https://www.hrw.org/news/2018/03/05/chinas-win-win-resolution-anything, Accessed on 9 July 2019

14 Logan Pauley, 'China Takes the Lead in UN Peacekeeping', *The Diplomat*, 17 April 2018, https://thediplomat.com/2018/04/china-takes-the-lead-in-un-peacekeeping/

15 Ibid.

16 'Families of Interpol Targets Harassed', Human Rights Watch, 31 January 2018, https://www.hrw.org/news/2018/01/31/china-families-interpol-targets-harassed, Accessed on 9 July 2019

17 An Baijie, 'WHO, China sign pact establishing "health Silk Road"', *China Daily*, 19 January 2017, http://www.chinadaily.com.cn/business/2017wef/2017-01/19/content_27993857.htm

18 Colum Lynch and Elias Groll, 'As US Retreats from World Organizations,

China Steps in to Fill the Void', 6 October 2017, https://foreignpolicy.com/2017/10/06/as-u-s-retreats-from-world-organizations-china-steps-in-the-fill-the-void/, Accessed on 9 July 2019

19 Ibid.

20 Timothy Health, 'China Prepares for an International Order After US Leadership', *Lawfare*, 1 August 2018, https://www.lawfareblog.com/china-prepares-international-order-after-us-leadership

21 Ibid.

22 Ibid.

23 'Hu Calls for enhancing "soft power" of Chinese culture', *Xinhua*, 15 October 2007, http://japanese.china.org.cn/english/congress/228142.htm, Accessed on 9 July 2019

24 'CCP Central Committee Resolution Concerning Some Major Issues in Comprehensively Deepening Reform', China Copyright and Media Blog, November 2013, https://chinacopyrightandmedia.wordpress.com/2013/11/15/ccp-central-committee-resolution-concerning-some-major-issues-in-comprehensively-deepening-reform/

25 Naoko Eto, 'China's Quest for Huayu Quan: Can Xi Jinping Change the Terms of International Discourse?', Tokyo Foundation for Policy Research, 4 October 2017, https://www.tkfd.or.jp/en/research/detail.php?id=663

26 'Hu Calls for enhancing 'soft power' of Chinese culture', *Xinhua*, 15 October 2007, http://japanese.china.org.cn/english/congress/228142.htm, Accessed on 9 July 2019

27 'China to promote cultural soft power', *China Daily*, 1 January 2014, http://europe.chinadaily.com.cn/china/2014-01/01/content_17208364.htm, Accessed on 9 July 2019

28 James Kynge, Lucy Hornby and Jamil Anderlini, 'Inside China's Secret "Magic Weapon" for Worldwide Influence', *Financial Times*, 26 October 2017. https://www.ft.com/content/fb2b3934-b004-11e7-beba-5521c713abf4

29 'Full text of Xi Jinping's report at 19th CPC National Congress', *Xinhua*, 18 October 2017, http://www.chinadaily.com.cn/m/shandong/yantai/2017-11/04/content_34175088.htm

30 'The United Front Work Department: "Magic Weapon" at Home and Abroad', *China Brief*, 6 July 2017. https://jamestown.org/program/united-front-work-department-magic-weapon-home-abroad/

31 'China to merge state media broadcasting giants', 21 March 2018, https://news.cgtn.com/news/794d444f7a6b7a6333566d54/share_p.html

32 'Xi Jinping asks for "absolute loyalty" from Chinese state media', *The*

Guardian, 19 February 2016.

33 Anne Marie Brady, 'Magic Weapons: Chinese political influence activities under Xi Jinping', Paper presented at the conference on 'The corrosion of democracy under China's global influence', supported by the Taiwan Foundation for Democracy, and hosted in Arlington, Virginia, USA, 16–17 September 2017, https://www.wilsoncenter.org/sites/default/files/for_website_magicweaponsanne-mariesbradyseptember2017.pdf

34 Emily Feng, 'China and the world: how Beijing spreads the message', *Financial Times*, 12 July 2018, https://www.ft.com/content/f5d00a86-3296-11e8-b5bf-23cb17fd1498, Accessed on 9 July 2019

35 Sarah Cook, 'Resisting Beijing's Global Media Influence', *The Diplomat*, 10 December 2015. http://thediplomat.com/2015/12/ resisting-beijings-global-media-influence/, Accessed on 9 July 2019

36 Javier C. Hernandez, 'Leading Western Publisher Bows to Chinese Censorship', *The New York Times*, 1 November 2017, available at https:// www.nytimes.com/2017/11/01/world/asia/china-springer-naturecensorship.html, accessed on 18 February 2018.

37 Tom Phillips, 'Cambridge University censorship U-turn is censored by China', *The Guardian*, 22 August 2017, https://www.theguardian.com/world/2017/aug/22/cambridge-university-censorship-u-turn-china

38 David Shambaugh, 'China's Soft Power Push', *Foreign Affairs*, July 2015, https://www.foreignaffairs.com/articles/china/2015-06-16/china-s-soft-power-push

39 'Criticizing Confucius Institutes', National Association of Scholars, 1 March 2019, https://www.nas.org/blogs/dicta/criticizing_confucius_institutes, Accessed on 9 July 2019

40 'A message from Confucius', *The Economist*, 24 October 2009, https://www.economist.com/special-report/2009/10/24/a-message-from-confucius

41 'Xi Jinping made important instructions on overseas Chinese affairs work: Concentrate on overseas Chinese and share the Chinese dream', *Peoples Daily*, 18 February 2017, http://cpc.people.com.cn/n1/2017/0218/c64094-29090242.html

42 Clive Hamilton and Alex Joske, 'Review of the National Security Legislation Amendment (Espionage and Foreign Interference) Bill 2017, Submission 20,' Parliament of Australia, 22 January 2018, https://www.aph.gov.au/DocumentStore.ashx?id=96afcef1-c6ea-4052-b5e3-bcac4951bb0e&subId=562658, Accessed on 9 July 2019

43 'Xi calls on world political parties to build community with shared future for mankind', *Xinhua*, 2 December 2017, http://www.xinhuanet.com//

english/2017-12/02/c_136794028.htm

44 Sam Coates, 'David Cameron cleared to lead £750m China trade fund', *The Times*, 18 December 2017, https://www.thetimes.co.uk/article/david-cameron-cleared-to-lead-750m-china-trade-fund-8fpgr2hpb

45 John Fitzgerald, 'How Bob Carr became China's pawn', AFR, 8 November 2018, https://www.afr.com/policy/what-you-should-know-about-bob-carr-and-china-20181105-h17jic

46 David Shullman, 'Protect the Party: China's growing influence in the developing world', Brookings Institution, 22 January 2019, https://www.brookings.edu/articles/protect-the-party-chinas-growing-influence-in-the-developing-world/

47 'Sharp Power: Rising Authoritarian Influence': New Forum Report, National Endowment for Democracy, 5 December 2017, https://www.ned.org/sharp-power-rising-authoritarian-influence-forum-report/

48 John Garnaut, 'The Reset', *The Monthly*, 1 August 2018, https://www.themonthly.com.au/issue/2018/august/1533045600/john-garnaut/australia-s-china-reset, Accessed on 9 July 2019

49 Luke Henriques Gomes, 'Nearly 80 per cent of foreign political donations come from China, data shows', *New Daily*, 10 December 2017, https://thenewdaily.com.au/news/national/2017/12/10/chinese-donations-australia/, Accessed on 9 July 2019

50 'Sam Dastayari resignation, How we got here', *ABC News*, 12 December 2017, https://www.abc.net.au/news/2017-12-12/sam-dastyari-resignation-how-did-we-get-here/9249380

51 Kelsey Munro, 'Australia's new foreign-influence laws: Who is targeted', *Lowy Interpreter*, 5 December 2018, https://www.lowyinstitute.org/the-interpreter/australia-new-foreign-influence-laws-who-targeted

52 'Australian state of Victoria signs MoU with China on Belt & Road', *China Daily*, 29 October 2018, https://bbs.chinadaily.com.cn/forum.php?mod=viewthread&tid=1895295, Accessed on 9 July 2019

53 See generally, 'Chinese interference: Anne-Marie Brady's full submission', *Newsroom*,8 May 2019, https://www.newsroom.co.nz/2019/05/08/575479/anne-marie-bradys-full-submission

54 'The Central Conference on Work Relating to Foreign Affairs Was Held in Beijing', 29 November 2011, MFAPRC, https://www.fmprc.gov.cn/mfa_eng/zxxx_662805/t1215680.shtml, Accessed on 9 July 2019

55 'The 4th Conference on Interaction and Confidence Building Measures in Asia (CICA) Summit Held in Shanghai Xi Jinping Presides over the Summit and Delivers Important Speech, Advocating Common, Comprehensive, Cooperative and Sustainable Security in Asia for New

Progress in Security Cooperation of Asia', Ministry of Foreign Affairs, Peoples Republic of China, 21 May 2014, https://www.fmprc.gov.cn/mfa_eng/topics_665678/yzxhxzyxrcshydscfh/t1162057.shtml

56 'Xi calls for overall national security outlook', *Xinhua*, 17 February 2017, http://www.xinhuanet.com/english/2017-02/17/c_136065190.htm

57 'Rising China Sells More Weapons', Federation of American Scientists, 3 May 2019, https://fas.org/blogs/secrecy/2019/05/china-weapons/

58 Sabine Mokry, 'How the Belt and Road Initiative globalizes China's national security policy', *Merics*, 15 November 2016, https://www.merics.org/en/blog/how-belt-and-road-initiative-globalizes-chinas-national-security-policy, Accessed on 9 July 2019

59 'Speech by Xi Jinping on neighbourhood policy to the Working Conference on Neighbourhood Relations', *Xinhua*, 25 October 2013, http://news.xinhuanet.com/politics/2013-10/25/c_117878944. htm

60 Graeme Smith, 'Chinese military bases in Vanuatu', Australian National University, 25 June 2018, http://asiapacific.anu.edu.au/news-events/all-stories/chinese-military-bases-vanuatu

61 Minnie Chan, 'First Djibouti now Pakistan port earmarked for Chinese overseas naval base, sources say', *South China Morning Post*, https://www.scmp.com/news/china/diplomacy-defence/article/2127040/first-djibouti-now-pakistan-port-earmarked-chinese, Accessed on 9 July 2019

62 'Xi Jinping: Further Creating a New Situation of Military Diplomacy', *Xinhua*, 29 January, 2015, http://cpc.people.com.cn/n/2015/0129/c64094-26474947.html

63 'Full Text: China's National Defence in the New Era', *Xinhua*, 24 July 2019, http://www.xinhuanet.com/english/2019-07/24/c_138253389.htm

64 'China-Africa defence, security forum opens in Beijing', *Xinhua*, 26 June 2018, http://www.xinhuanet.com/english/2018-06/26/c_137282618.htm

65 Elizabeth Economy, *The Third Revoluton: Xi Jinping and the New Chinese State*, Oxford University Press, 3 May 2018.

66 Laura Zhou, 'China embarks on first joint naval drills with Asean as US tensions simmer in South China Sea', SCMP, 22 October 2018, https://www.scmp.com/news/china/military/article/2169727/china-embarks-first-joint-naval-drills-asean-us-tensions-simmer

67 'Military and Security Developments Involving the People's Republic of China 2018', Office of the Secretary of Defence, 16 May 2018, https://media.defence.gov/2018/Aug/16/2001955282/-1/-1/1/2018-CHINA-MILITARY-POWER-REPORT.PDF, pp. 31.

68 Rajeev Chaturvedy, 'The Beijing Xiangshan Forum: Competition or Co-

existence?', *RSIS Commentaries*, 19 November 2018, https://www.rsis.edu.sg/rsis-publication/rsis/the-beijing-xiangshan-forum-competition-or-co-existence/#.XVZd5JMzZN0

69 Andrew Osborn, 'Russia starts biggest war games since Soviet fall near China', Reuters, 11 September 2018, https://www.reuters.com/article/us-russia-exercises-vostok/russia-starts-biggest-war-games-since-soviet-fall-near-china-idUSKCN1LR146

70 'China, Russia naval drill in South China Sea to begin Monday', Reuters, 11 September, 2016, https://www.reuters.com/article/us-southchinasea-china-russia-idUSKCN11H051

71 Rodion Ebbighausen, 'China and Russia combine naval forces in the Baltic Sea', DW, 24 July 2017, https://www.dw.com/en/china-and-russia-combine-naval-forces-in-the-baltic-sea/a-39816926

72 Andrew Osborn and Joyce Lee, 'First Russian-Chinese air patrol in Asia-Pacific draws shots from South Korea', Reuters, 23 July 2019, https://www.reuters.com/article/us-southkorea-russia-aircraft/first-russian-chinese-air-patrol-in-asia-pacific-draws-shots-from-south-korea-idUSKCN1UI072

73 Oki Nagai and Tomoyo Ogawa, 'Xi-Putin summit in Vladivostok highlights common front against US', *Nikkei Asian Review*, 11 September 2018, https://asia.nikkei.com/Politics/International-relations/Xi-Putin-summit-in-Vladivostok-highlights-common-front-against-US2

74 'China will take a more active role in world problems, Xi Jinping says', *South China Morning Post*, 1 December 2017, https://www.scmp.com/news/china/policies-politics/article/2122536/china-will-take-more-active-role-world-problems-xi, Accessed on 9 July 2019

CHAPTER VIII: THREE COLLISIONS AND THE END OF THE LIBERAL WORLD ORDER

1 David Sanger, 'Strange New Land: America in a Time of Trump', *The New York Times*, 9 November 2016, https://www.nytimes.com/2016/11/10/us/politics/donald-trump-presidential-agenda.html , Accessed 10 July 2019

2 'Is the Liberal Order in Peril', *Foreign Affairs*, https://www.foreignaffairs.com/ask-the-experts/liberal-order-peril, Accessed 10 July 2019

3 'Global Trends Report, Paradox of Progress', US National Intelligence Council, January 2017, https://www.dni.gov/index.php/global-trends-home, Accessed 10 July 2019

4 This section is based almost entirely on an existing piece written by Samir Saran for the World Economic Forum. https://www.weforum.org/agenda/2018/11/eurasia-indo-pacific-arctic-new-world-order/

5 The Atlantic Conference & Charter, 1941, Office of the Historian, Department of State, https://history.state.gov/milestones/1937-1945/atlantic-conf

6 Walter Lippmann, *US Foreign Policy: Shield of the Republic*, Boston, 1943, pp. 135

7 'Confluence of the Two Seas', Speech by H.E.Mr Shinzo Abe, Prime Minister of Japan at the Parliament of the Republic of India, Ministry of Foreign Affairs, Japan, 22 August 2007, https://www.mofa.go.jp/region/asia-paci/pmv0708/speech-2.html

8 Zbigniew Brzezinski, 'A Geostrategy for Eurasia', *Foreign Affairs*, September 1997, https://www.foreignaffairs.com/articles/asia/1997-09-01/geostrategy-eurasia

9 'Arctic Shipping Route Will Soon Rival Suez Canal, Putin Says', *Yale Environment* 360, 23 September 2011, https://e360.yale.edu/digest/arctic_shipping_route_will_soon_rival_suez_canal_putin_says, Accessed 10 July 2019

10 Eric Schmidt and Jared Cohen, *New Digital Age: Reshaping the Future of People, Nations and Business*, John Murray, 2013.

11 'There are now over 3 billion social media users in the world—about 40 per cent of the global population', Mashable, 7 August 2017, https://mashable.com/2017/08/07/3-billion-global-social-media-users/

12 Olivia Solon and Sabrina Siddiqui, 'Russia-backed Facebook posts "reached 126m Americans" during US election', *The Guardian*, 31 October 2017, https://www.theguardian.com/technology/2017/oct/30/facebook-russia-fake-accounts-126-million

13 *The Theft Of American Intellectual Property: Reassessment of the Challenge And United States Policy*, I.P. Commission Report, 2017, http://ipcommission.org/report/IP_Commission_Report_Update_2017.pdf, Accessed 10 July 2019

14 'Twitter blocks accounts of Iranian state media outlets', *France24*, 20 July 2019, https://www.france24.com/en/20190720-twitter-blocks-accounts-iranian-state-media-outlets

15 Rita Liao and Manish Singh, 'GitHub confirms it has blocked developers in Iran, Syria and Crimea', *Tech Crunch*, 29 July 2019, https://techcrunch.com/2019/07/29/github-ban-sanctioned-countries/

16 Daron Acemoglu et al, 'The rise of China and the Future of US Manufacturing', *VoxEU*, 28 September 2014, https://voxeu.org/article/

rise-china-and-future-us-manufacturing, Accessed 10 July 2019

17 'Poorer Than Their Parents?', McKinsey Global Institute, July 2016, https://www.mckinsey.com/~/media/mckinsey/featured%20insights/Employment%20and%20Growth/Poorer%20than%20their%20parents%20A%20new%20perspective%20on%20income%20inequality/MGI-Income%20-Inequality-Executive-summary-July-2016.ashx

18 'Transcript: Donald Trump's Foreign Policy Speech', *The New York Times*, 27 April 2016, https://www.nytimes.com/2016/04/28/us/politics/transcript-trump-foreign-policy.html, Accessed 10 July 2019

19 For context on this initiative, see Scott Kennedy, 'Made in China 2025', CSIS, https://www.csis.org/analysis/made-china-2025, Accessed 10 July 2019

20 Richard Hass, 'Liberal World Order, R.I.P', CFR, 21 March 2018, https://www.cfr.org/article/liberal-world-order-rip

21 Max Roser, 'Democracy', Our World in Data, June 2019, https://ourworldindata.org/democracy

CHAPTER IX: XI DREAMS

1 Rupert Wingfield-Hayes, 'Japan accuses China of airspace intrusion over islands' BBC News, 13 December 2012, http://www.bbc.co.uk/news/world-asia-20707760

2 Shivshankar Menon, 'What China's rise means for the world' *The Wire,* 2 January 2016, https://thewire.in/external-affairs/what-chinas-rise-means-for-the-world

3 Xi Jinping, 'Secure a Decisive Victory in Building a Moderately Prosperous Society in All Respects and Strive for the Great Success of Socialism with Chinese Characteristics for a New Era' (Speech, Beijing, 18 October 2017), *Xinhua,* http://www.xinhuanet.com/english/special/2017-11/03/c_136725942.htm

4 Tom Phillips, 'This could destroy China: parliament sets Xi Jinping up to rule for life', *The Guardian,* 11 March 2018, https://www.theguardian.com/world/2018/mar/11/this-could destroy-china-parliament-sets-xi-jinping-up-to-rule-for-life

5 Kerry Allen, 'China censorship after Xi Jinping presidency extension proposal', BBC, 26 February 2018, http://www.bbc.com/news/world-asia-china-43198404

6 Bethany Allen-Ebrahimian, 'Chinese students in America say "Not My President"', *Foreign Policy,* 7 March 2018, http://foreignpolicy.

com/2018/03/07/chinese-students-in-america-say-not-my-president-xi-jinping-china/

7 Ibid.

8 Kevin Liptak, 'Trump on China's Xi consolidating power: "Maybe we'll give that a shot someday"', CNN, 4 March 2018, https://edition.cnn.com/2018/03/03/politics/trump-maralago-remarks/index.html

9 Taisu Zhang, 'Maybe the Law Does Actually Matter to Xi Jinping', *ChinaFile,* 1 March 2018, http://www.chinafile.com/reporting-opinion/viewpoint/maybe-law-does-actually-matter-xi-jinping

10 Xi Jinping, 'Achieving Rejuvenation Is the Dream of the Chinese People', as available in Xi Jinping, *The Governance of China*, Volume I (Beijing: Foreign Languages Press Co., 2014), p. 107.

11 Xu Lingui, 'China embraces new "principal contradiction" when embarking on new journey', *Xinhua,* 20 October 2017, http://www.xinhuanet.com/english/2017-10/20/c_136694592.htm

12 Ibid.

13 China Overview, World Bank, http://www.worldbank.org/en/country/china/overview

14 Global Innovation Index 2017 Report, https://www.globalinnovationindex.org/

15 Joshua Keating, 'China Claims Title of World's Top Trading Nation', *Slate,* 13 January 2014, http://www.slate.com/blogs/the_world_/2014/01/13/china_claims_title_of_world_s_top_trading_nation.html

16 Rajeshwari Pillai Rajagopalan, 'China's 2018 Military Budget: New Numbers, Old Worries', *The Diplomat,* 7 March 2018

17 Shannon Tiezzi, 'Report: China's 1 Per cent Owns 1/3 of Wealth', *The Diplomat,* 15 January 2016, https://thediplomat.com/2016/01/report-chinas-1-percent-owns-13-of-wealth/

18 Country Profile: China, Transparency International, Corruption Perception Index 2017, https://www.transparency.org/country/CHN

19 Richard Wike and Bridget Parker, 'Corruption, Pollution, Inequality are Top Concerns in China', Pew Research Center, 25 September 2015, http://www.pewglobal.org/2015/09/24/corruption-pollution-inequality-are-top-concerns-in-china/

20 Indira P. Ravindran, 'Key takeaways from Xi's work report', *Gateway House,* 23 October 2017, http://www.gatewayhouse.in/xis-work-report/

21 'Xi Jinping has more clout than Donald Trump. The world should be wary', *The Economist,* 14 October 2017, https://www.economist.com/news/leaders/21730144-do-not-expect-mr-xi-change-china-or-world-better-xi-jinping-has-more-clout

22 Benjamin Hass, 'Xi Jinping makes China's toilets a number two priority', *The Guardian,* 28 November 2017, https://www.theguardian.com/world/2017/nov/28/xi-jinping-makes-chinas-toilets-a-number-two-priority

23 Alan Wheatley, 'Too soon to call time on China's economy boom', Reuters, 23 May 2011, https://www.reuters.com/article/idINIndia-57213520110523

24 'Moody's: China's consolidation of power could advance economic rebalancing, though challenges remain', Moody's Investor Services, 27 October 2017, https://www.moodys.com/research/Moodys-Chinas-consolidation-of-power-could-advance-economic-rebalancing-though--PR_374543

25 Qian Gang, 'The Tea Leaves of Xi-Era Discourse', *China Media Project,* 14 November 2017, http://chinamediaproject.org/2017/11/14/the-tea-leaves-of-xi-era-discourse/

26 'Hu Jintao: Promote Comprehensive Party Building in the Spirit of Reform and Innovation', *Xinhua,* 15 October 2011, quoted in Cheng Li, *Chinese Politics in the Xi Jinping Era* (Washington, DC: The Brookings Institution), p.13.

27 Deng Xiaoping, *Deng Xiaoping wenxuan [Selected works of Deng Xiaoping],* Vol. 3 (Beijing: Renmin chubanshe, 1993), 365, quoted in Cheng Li, *Chinese Politics in the Xi Jinping Era* (Washington, DC: The Brookings Institution), p. 13.

28 Cheng Li and Eve Cary, 'The Last Year of Hu's Leadership: Hu's to Blame?' *China Brief,* Volume 11, Issue 23, 2011, https://jamestown.org/program/the-last-year-of-hus-leadership-hus-to-blame/

29 Douglas Yeung and Astrid Stuth Chevallos, 'The Mountains Are High and the Emperor Is Far Away', *Foreign Policy,* 11 November 2014, http://foreignpolicy.com/2014/11/11/the-mountains-are-high-and-the-emperor-is-far-away/

30 Katsuji Nakazawa, 'Xi Jinping's next goal? Communist Party chairman for life', *Nikkei Asian Review,* 27 February 2018, https://asia.nikkei.com/Editor-s-Picks/China-up-close/Xi-Jinping-s-next-goal-Communist-Party-chairman-for-life

31 Willy Wo-Lap Lam, 'The Eclipse of the Communist Youth League and the Rise of the Zehjiang Clique', Jamestown Foundation, 11 May 2016, https://jamestown.org/program/the-eclipse-of-the-communist-youth-league-and-the-rise-of-the-zhejiang-clique/#.V-1Xq_krK71

32 Andrew S. Erickson, 'Sweeping Changes in China's Military: Xi's PLA Restructuring', *The Wall Street Journal,* 2 September 2015, https://

blogs.wsj.com/chinarealtime/2015/09/02/sweeping-change-in-chinas-military-xis-pla-restructuring/

33 Katsuji Nakazawa, 'Xi tells his troops: "Call me chairman"', *Nikkei Asian Review,* 10 July 2017, https://asia.nikkei.com/Politics/Xi-tells-his-troops-Call-me-chairman

34 Elizabeth C. Economy, *The Third Revolution: Xi Jinping and the New Chinese State* (New York: Oxford University Press, 2018), p.5.

35 Lu Hui, 'Commentary: Milestone congress points to new era for China, the world', *Xinhua,* 24 October 2017, http://www.xinhuanet.com/english/2017-10/24/c_136702090.htm

36 Yurou, 'Facts and Figures about China's major country diplomacy: global trotting President Xi', *Xinhua,* 6 September 2017, http://www.xinhuanet.com/english/2017-09/06/c_136589556.htm

37 Elizabeth Economy, 'China's New Revolution, The Reign of Xi Jinping', *Foreign Affairs,* May 2018, https://www.foreignaffairs.com/articles/china/2018-04-17/chinas-new-revolution

38 Howard French, *Everything under the Heavens, How the Past Helps Shape China's Push for Global Power,* New York: Scribe, 2017, p.3.

39 Xi Jinping, 'Zai jinian Zhongguo renmin kangri zhanzheng ji shijie fan faxisi zhanzheng shengli 70 zhounian zhaodaihuishang de jianghua', *Xinhua*, 3 September 2015, quoted in Alison Kaufman, 'Xi Jinping as Historian: Marxist, Chinese, Nationalist, Global', *The Asan Forum,* 15 October 2015, http://www.theasanforum.org/xi-jinping-as-historian-marxist-chinese-nationalist-global/

40 Timothy R. Heath, 'What does the 19th Party Congress mean for the PLA', RAND Corporation, 18 October 2017, https://www.rand.org/blog/2017/10/what-does-the-19th-party-congress-mean-for-the-pla.html

41 Vice Admiral Anil Chopra, 'Xi's PLA Agenda: real reform or power gambit?', *Gateway House,* 12 October 2017, http://www.gatewayhouse.in/xi-pla-agenda/?utm_source=MadMimi&utm_medium=email&utm_content=Xi%E2%80%99s+PLA+agenda%3A+real+reform+or+power+gambit%3F+%7C+IMF%2C+WB+Annual+Meetings+2017%3A+growth+outlook+%7C+Russia_India+Energy+Cooperation%3A+Trade%2C+Joint+Projects%2C+and+New+Areas+%7C+Discussing+river+preservation&utm_campaign=20171005_m141910929_Weekly+Briefing+2017&utm_term=Read+more

42 Admiral Harry Harris Jr., Commander, US Pacific Command, Statement before the House Committee on Armed Services, 14 February 2018, https://armedservices.house.gov/legislation/hearings/military-and-security-challenges-and-posture-indo-pacific-region

43 Samantha Raphelson, 'The Taiwan Travel Act Threeatens to Further Complicate US, China Relations', *NPR,* 10 April 2018, https://www.npr.org/2018/04/10/601215534/the-taiwan-travel-act-threatens-to-further-complicate-u-s-china-relations

44 Minnie Chan, 'China announces surprise live fire Taiwan Strait drills after massive military parade', *South China Morning Post,* 12 April 2018, http://www.scmp.com/news/china/diplomacy-defence/article/2141505/surprise-move-china-mount-live-fire-navy-drills-taiwan

45 Graham Allison, *Destined for War: Can America and China Escape The Thucydides's Trap?,* New York: Houghton Mifflin Harcourt, 2017.

46 Xi Jinping, 'Work Together to Build the Silk Road Economic Belt', in Xi Jinping, *The Governance of China*, Volume I (Beijing: Foreign Languages Press Co., 2014) p. 653.

47 'Wang Yi Talks about the Essence of Major Country Diplomacy with Chinese Characteristics: To Promote More Countries' Understanding and Recognition of Socialism Path with Chinese Characteristics', Ministry of Foreign Affairs of the Peoples Republic of China, 19 October 2017, http://www.fmprc.gov.cn/mfa_eng/zxxx_662805/t1503756.shtml

48 Go Yamada and Stefania Palma, 'Is China's Belt and Road working? A progress report from eight countries', *Nikkei Asian Review,* 28 March 2018, https://asia.nikkei.com/Spotlight/Cover-Story/Is-China-s-Belt-and-Road-working-A-progress-report-from-eight-countries

49 Ibid.

50 Speech delivered by former Secretary of State Rex Tillerson, 'Defining Our Relationship with India for the Next Century', at the Centre for Strategic and International Studies, 18 October 2017, https://www.csis.org/events/defining-our-relationship-india-next-century-address-us-secretary-state-rex-tillerson/

51 Simon Denyer, 'China sets up new foreign aid agency to better project influence abroad', *The Washington Post,* 13 March 2018, https://www.washingtonpost.com/world/china-promotes-foreign-aid-bolsters-environment-ministry-in-government-shake-up/2018/03/13/d3c26d94-267a-11e8-ab19-06a445a08c94_story.html?utm_term=.fe29269f060a

52 Alvin Camba, 'The Philippines Chinese FDI boom: more politics than geopolitics', *New Mandala,* 30 January 2018, http://www.newmandala.org/duterte-philippines-chinese-investment-boom-politics-geopolitics/

53 Thorsten Benner and Jan Weidenfeld, 'Europe, don't let China divide and conquer', *Politico,* 19 March 2018, https://www.politico.eu/article/europe-china-divide-and-conquer/

54 Dinakar Peri, 'China's rise a big disruption, says Jaishankar', *The Hindu,*

18 January 2018, http://www.thehindu.com/news/national/chinas-rise-a-big-disruption-says-jaishankar/article22466659.ece

55 'Wang Yi Talks about the Essence of Major Country Diplomacy with Chinese Characteristics: To Promote More Countries' Understanding and Recognition of Socialism Path with Chinese Characteristics', Ministry of Foreign Affairs of the Peoples Republic of China, 19 October 2017, http://www.fmprc.gov.cn/mfa_eng/zxxx_662805/t1503756.shtml

56 Elizabeth Economy, 'China's New Revolution, The Reign of Xi Jinping', *Foreign Affairs,* May 2018, https://www.foreignaffairs.com/articles/china/2018-04-17/chinas-new-revolution

57 Fu Ying, 'How China Sees Russia', *Foreign Affairs*, January/February 2016, https://www.foreignaffairs.com/articles/china/2015-12-14/howchina-sees-russia

58 PM's statement on 'Creating a shared future in a Fractured World' in World Economic Forum Summit, Davos, 23 January 2018, http://www.pmindia.gov.in/en/news_updates/pms-address-at-world-economic-forum-in-davos-on-the-theme-creating-a-shared-future-in-a-fractured-world/?comment=disable

59 Text of PM's thirty-seventh Singapore Lecture 'India's Singapore Story' during his visit to Singapore, 23 November 2015, http://www.pmindia.gov.in/en/news_updates/text-of-37th-singapore-lecture-indias-singapore-story-by-prime-minister-during-his-visit-to-singapore/

60 Speech by the foreign secretary at Raisina Dialogue in New Delhi, Ministry of External Affairs, 2 March 2016, http://mea.gov.in/Speeches-Statements.htm?dtl/26433

61 Ibid.

62 Colonel Vinayak Bhat, 'New trouble for India: China occupies North Doklam, with armoured vehicles and 7 helipads', *The Print,* 17 January 2018, https://theprint.in/security/new-trouble-for-india-as-china-fully-occupies-doklam/29561/

63 Sanjeev Miglani and Ben Blanchard, 'India and China agree to end border standoff', Reuters, 28 August 2017, https://www.reuters.com/article/us-india-china/india-and-china-agree-to-end-border-standoff-idUSKCN1B80II

64 Robert A. Manning and Bharat Gopalaswamy, 'Is Abdulla Yameen Handing Over the Maldives to China?' *Foreign Policy,* 21 March 2018, http://foreignpolicy.com/2018/03/21/is-abdulla-yameen-handing-over-the-maldives-to-china/

65 'Chinese warships enter East Indian Ocean amid Maldives tensions', Reuters, 20 February 2018, https://www.reuters.com/article/us-

maldives-politics-china/chinese-warships-enter-east-indian-ocean-amid-maldives-tensions-idUSKCN1G40V9

66 N. Manasa Mohan, 'Boat ride, walks and talks: Modi's two days at Wuhan', *Hindustan Times,* 28 April 2017, https://www.hindustantimes.com/india-news/boat-ride-walks-and-talks-modi-s-two-days-in-wuhan/story-tzFn98qajkumsfA6IrrcpJ.html

67 Abantika Gosh, 'Govt sends out note: Very sensitive time for ties with China, so skip Dalai Lama events', *The Indian Express,* 2 March 2018, http://indianexpress.com/article/india/govt-sends-out-note-very-sensitive-time-for-ties-with-china-so-skip-dalai-lama-events-5083430/

68 Jyoti Malhotra, 'Stepping back from Maldives, India tells China', *The Indian Express,* 28 March 2018, http://indianexpress.com/article/india/stepping-back-from-maldives-india-to-china-doklam-5113855/

69 Zeeshaan Shaikh, 'China responds: Dragon and elephant must not fight, but dance together', *The Indian Express,* 9 March 2018, http://indianexpress.com/article/world/china-responds-dragon-and-elephant-must-not-fight-but-dance-together-5091470/

70 Mihir Sharma, 'Asia's Imbalance of Power', Bloomberg, 27 April 2018, https://www.bloomberg.com/view/articles/2018-04-26/power-imbalance-between-india-and-china-has-grown-lopsided

71 Sreeram Chaulia, 'Trump is Driving Xi Into Modi's Arms', *Foreign Policy,* 27 April 2018, https://foreignpolicy.com/2018/04/27/trump-is-driving-xi-into-modis-arms/

72 Prime Minister's Office, 'PM issues statement before his departure to China', Press Information Bureau, 26 April 2018, http://pib.nic.in/PressReleaseIframePage.aspx?PRID=1530379

73 Bruce Stokes, Dorothy Macevich and Hanyi Chwe, 'India and the world', Pew Research Center, 15 November 2017, http://www.pewglobal.org/2017/11/15/india-and-the-world/Xi

74 Josh Chin, 'China spends more on domestic security as Xi's power grow', *The Wall Street Journal,* 6 March 2018, https://www.wsj.com/articles/china-spends-more-on-domestic-security-as-xis-powers-grow-1520358522

75 'Summary of the National Defence Strategy of the United States of America, 2018', United States Department of Defence, 19 January 2018, https://www.defence.gov/News/Article/Article/1419045/dod-official-national-defence-strategy-will-rebuild-dominance-enhance-deterrence/

EPILOGUE

1 See generally, Scott B. Macdonald, China and India: Same Globalization Road, Different Destinies, Yale Global, 24 October 2007, https://yaleglobal.yale.edu/content/china-and-india-same-globalization-road-different-destinies

2 S. Jaishankar, 'Is nationalism the new normal and can India make a difference–by being different?', Full text of the speech by foreign secretary at Second Raisina Dialogue in New Delhi, *Scroll*, 18 January 2017, https://scroll.in/article/827030/is-nationalism-the-new-normal-and-can-india-make-a-difference-by-being-different-s-jaishankar

3 Samir Saran, 'World in flux: India's choices may help manage disruptions', ORF, 25 January 2018, https://www.orfonline.org/expert-speak/world-flux-india-choices-may-help-manage-disruptions/

4 ''Issue-based alignments' may be the focus of Jaishankar's foreign policies', *Hindustan Times*, 2 June 2019, https://www.hindustantimes.com/india-news/issue-based-alignments-may-be-the-focus-of-jaishankar-s-foreign-policies/story-9kKT370c3iZWN4IgI3za6K.html

5 C. Raja Mohan, *India's Foreign Policy: Nehru's Enduring Legacy*, Oxford University Press, 3 October 2015, https://blog.oup.com/2015/10/india-foreign-policy-nehru-legacy/

6 Panel discussion, 'The World in a Moment: Looking Back, Looking Ahead, Looking Hard', Raisina Dialogue 2019, 9 January 2019, https://www.youtube.com/watch?v=FH2el8qEM4A

INDEX

1931
16.9.25